Navision & Dynamics NAV User Guide

Ruth Lestina

Navision Depot Press
www.navisiondepot.com

ISBN-13: 978-0615944913
ISBN-10: 0615944914

Table of Contents

Classic Nav: The Basics

Versions

The information in this manual applies to Dynamics Nav / Navision versions including 2.x, 3.x, 4.x, 5.x, and 2009 Classic Client. The Role Tailored Client versions, including RTC 2009 and 2013, look very different and while the basic functions are mostly the same, the navigation is totally different and so are the shortcut keys. While there have been some look and feel changes from version 2.x to 2009 Classic, the shortcut keys have not changed, and the basic layout and navigation also remain constant. Therefore, this manual will be helpful for any version from Navision 2.0 to Dynamics NAV 2009 Classic Client.

Saving Data

Nav saves data on a field by field basis. Therefore, there is no "save" button or function. As you enter data into any field, you need to be aware that as soon as you leave that field, either by tabbing out, or by clicking somewhere else, the data you entered will immediately be saved.

Undo Function

Nav does NOT have an undo function. Windows Ctrl+Z does not work. The closest thing Nav has to an undo function is this: if you start editing text in a field, and then hit the escape key without leaving that field, it will undo your changes and put back the text the way it was before. This only works within one field, and only if you hit escape after deleting or changing data but before hitting tab or clicking outside of the field you changed.

Audit Trails & Changing Posted Data

You cannot directly change posted data in Nav. This is good, because it means you have an audit trail of everything that happens, and you don't have to wonder why your numbers changed after you closed a fiscal period. However, it also means that if you are used to using less structured software, like Quickbooks, you will have to get used to having to post reversing entries rather than just deleting or changing old entries.

How to Use Filters to Find the Information You Need

Overview

Navision has very flexible and powerful filtering capabilities that will let you see just about any specific sub-set of data that you might want. There are two different types of filters: field/table filters, and flow filters. These work rather differently and can be used individually or in combination. Setting filters has very specific syntax in order to get the results you want. A list of common syntax formats you can use to make your filters work better is included. This section provides step-by-step instructions to show you how to use flow filters, field filters, and table filters in Dynamics Nav / Navision to find just the specific information you need..

Instructions: Filters in General

You can access the filters from the shortcut menu:

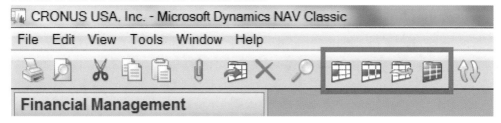

Or from the View menu, or by using the shortcut keys:

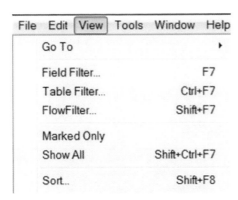

Instructions: Field/Table Filters

Field filters and table filters are basically the same thing. Field and table filters are designed to let you select a sub-set of your data to look at or work with, based on values in the data. You can set field or table filters in list view, or on a card.

1) To set field or table filters in list view, open up the list you want to see (usually by pressing F5 or clicking the List button). For example, open the customer list:

2) Then click on the field you want to filter on, for example, let's set a filter by location. Click on the location column, and press F7 or click the Field Filter button.

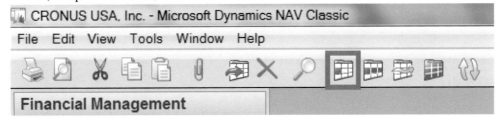

3) The Field Filter box will pop up, and it will automatically be populated with the value in the field that you had selected – in this case, "BLUE".

4) Either leave the filter value alone, or change it to whatever you want, then click OK to apply the filter. You can then see that the data in your list view is now limited to data that fit the filter – so in this case, you only see customers with a location value of "BLUE".

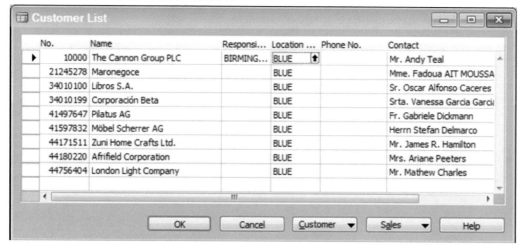

5) You can set additional filters to further limit the same data by clicking other fields and setting filters on them as well. These filters are cumulative. So we can for example set another filter on the Name field to show only those companies whose names start with the letter "M", as shown:

6) When we apply this filter, we will now see only customers with a location of "BLUE" and a name that starts with "M".

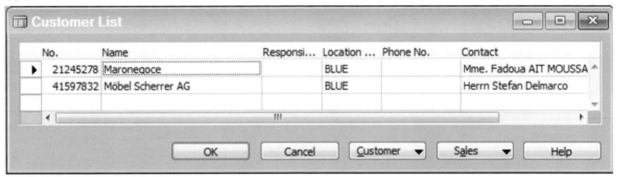

7) If at any point we get confused about what filters are set, or we simply want to change the filters from one central screen, we can use the table filter to see or change the filter set we are using. Click the table filter button or press Ctrl+F7.

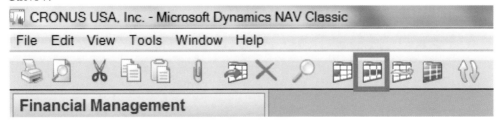

8) You'll see the specifics of what filters are currently applied, and you can set additional filters or make changes to the applied filters.

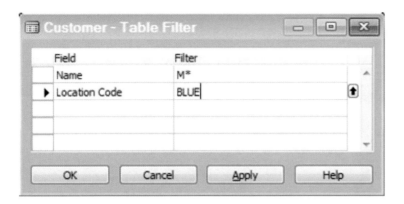

9) For example, we can broaden our location filter to show any customer with a location of "BLUE" or "YELLOW" by adding a "|" (pipe-through character, usually above the "\" on your keyboard) and then the additional value. Then click OK.

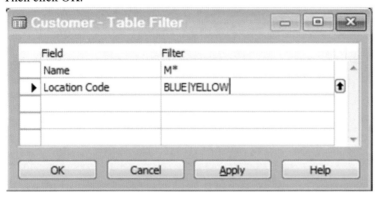

10) Then you'll see all customers with a location of "BLUE" or "YELLOW" and a name starting with the letter "M".

11) You can also use the table filter to add filters on fields that are not shown on the list view. So for example we can add a filter by Service Zone Code, even though that field is not available or visible in list view. Just click into an empty field on the left side of the table filter box, under the 'Field' heading, and type the field name or pick it from the list, then tab over and enter the value(s) to filter by. Then click OK to apply the filter.

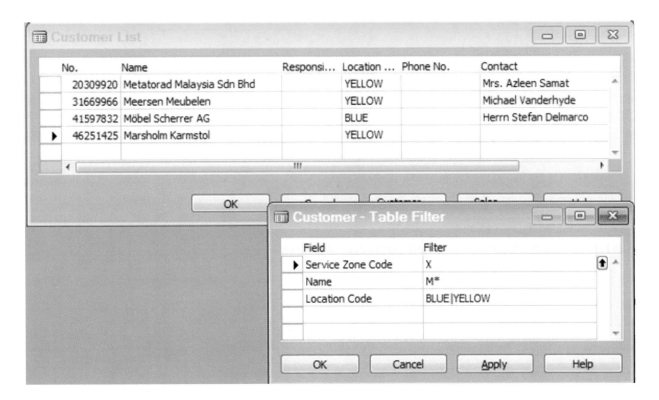

12) To remove all filters, press Shift+Ctrl+F7, Show All, or click the Show All button.

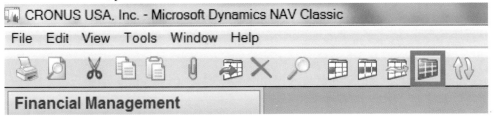

Instructions: Flow Filters

Flow filters are a special kind of filter that is designed to be used with ledger entry data, and that allows you to set limits on what data is included in calculated totals. For example, you use flow filters to show only data for the previous fiscal year in the general ledger.

1) To apply a flow filter, first open the ledger you want to look at, for example, the general ledger.

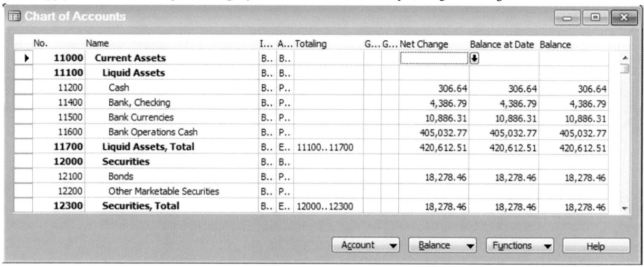

2) To apply the flow filter, push Shift+F7 or click the Flow Filter button.

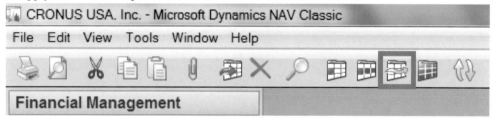

3) The Flow Filter box will pop up, and you can enter your filter criteria. For example, we want to see only the data from June 1, 2009 to June 30, 2009. So we enter 6/1/09..6/30/09 in the date filter and click apply or OK to see the changes. Note that now the net change and balance at date are based on the June dates supplied, while the balance is still the current date's balance.

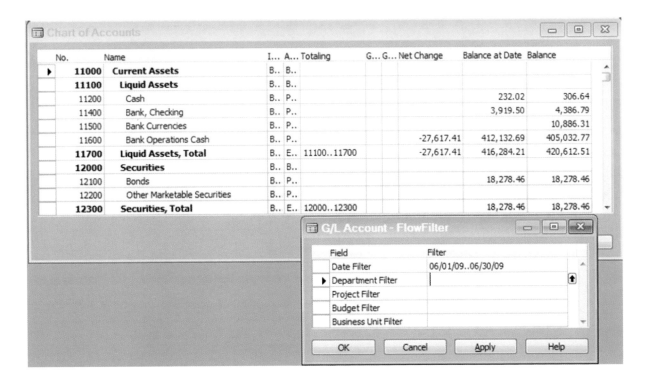

No.	Name	I...	A...	Totaling	G...	G...	Net Change	Balance at Date	Balance
11000	**Current Assets**	B..	B..						
11100	**Liquid Assets**	B..	B..						
11200	Cash	B..	P..					232.02	306.64
11400	Bank, Checking	B..	P..					3,919.50	4,386.79
11500	Bank Currencies	B..	P..						10,886.31
11600	Bank Operations Cash	B..	P..				-27,617.41	412,132.69	405,032.77
11700	**Liquid Assets, Total**	B..	E..	11100..11700			-27,617.41	416,284.21	420,612.51
12000	**Securities**	B..	B..						
12100	Bonds	B..	P..					18,278.46	18,278.46
12200	Other Marketable Securities	B..	P..						
12300	**Securities, Total**	B..	E..	12000..12300				18,278.46	18,278.46

G/L Account - FlowFilter

Field	Filter
Date Filter	06/01/09..06/30/09
▶ Department Filter	
Project Filter	
Budget Filter	
Business Unit Filter	

[OK]   [Cancel]   [Apply]   [Help]

4) You can also add table or field filters in the flow filter box. For example, let's say we want to see only income sheet accounts. Since that is not a calculated field, it's not a flow filter, but we can use the flow filter box to add it anyway. Scroll down to a blank line, and add a filter on income/balance, as shown:

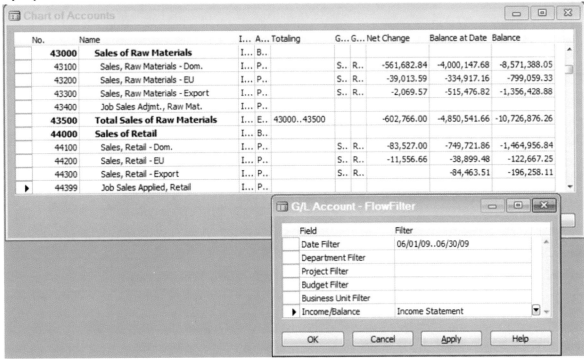

No.	Name	I...	A...	Totaling	G...	G...	Net Change	Balance at Date	Balance
43000	**Sales of Raw Materials**	I...	B..						
43100	Sales, Raw Materials - Dom.	I...	P..		S..	R..	-561,682.84	-4,000,147.68	-8,571,388.05
43200	Sales, Raw Materials - EU	I...	P..		S..	R..	-39,013.59	-334,917.16	-799,059.33
43300	Sales, Raw Materials - Export	I...	P..		S..	R..	-2,069.57	-515,476.82	-1,356,428.88
43400	Job Sales Adjmt., Raw Mat.	I...	P..						
43500	**Total Sales of Raw Materials**	I...	E..	43000..43500			-602,766.00	-4,850,541.66	-10,726,876.26
44000	**Sales of Retail**	I...	B..						
44100	Sales, Retail - Dom.	I...	P..		S..	R..	-83,527.00	-749,721.86	-1,464,956.84
44200	Sales, Retail - EU	I...	P..		S..	R..	-11,556.66	-38,899.48	-122,667.25
44300	Sales, Retail - Export	I...	P..		S..	R..		-84,463.51	-196,258.11
▶ 44399	Job Sales Applied, Retail	I...	P..						

G/L Account - FlowFilter

Field	Filter
Date Filter	06/01/09..06/30/09
Department Filter	
Project Filter	
Budget Filter	
Business Unit Filter	
▶ Income/Balance	Income Statement

[OK]   [Cancel]   [Apply]   [Help]

5) You'll see in the data that both the date flow filter and the field income/balance filter have been applied. If you re-open the flow filter box, however, the income/balance filter will not be visible – but if you click the table filter box, you'll see it.

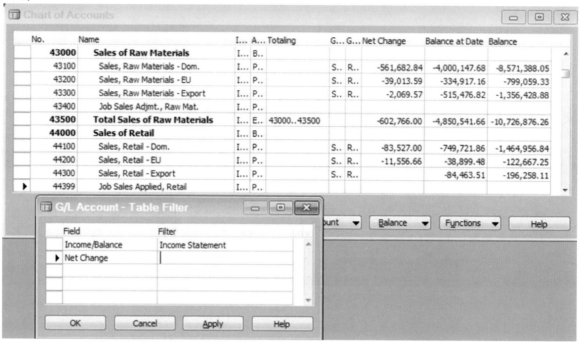

6) Note that Show All will clear table or field filters, but it DOES NOT clear flow filters. To remove a flow filter, you have to click the flow filter button or push Shift+F7, remove the filter, and then click OK – essentially set all the flow filters to blank.

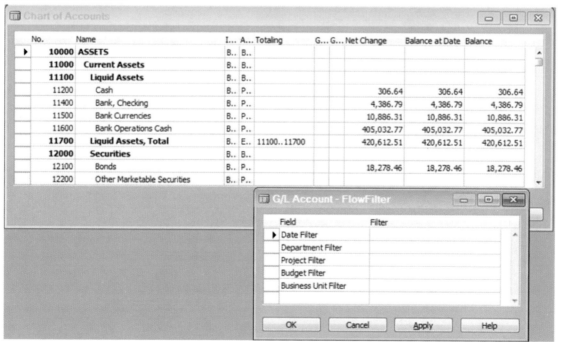

Instructions: Filter Syntax

Setting filters has very specific syntax in order to get the results you want. Here are many common syntax formats you can use to make your filters work better.

Filter Purpose	Example	Results
From date to date	01/01/2010..01/31/2010	Everything with a date between Jan 1st and Jan 31st 2010
Prior to and including date	..12/31/2009	Everything with a date before or on Dec 31st 2009, but nothing afterwards
After and including date	01/01/2010..	Everything with a date on or after Jan 1st 2010 but nothing before
Only on date	12/31/2009	Only records with a date specifically on Dec 31st 2009
Specific Text, case sensitive	TEST	Only records with the word TEST and nothing else; won't find Test, or test, or TEST RECORD
Specific Text, not case sensitive	@TEST	The '@' means ignore case; will find TEST or Test or test, but not Test Record or New Test
Starts with Text, case sensitive	Test*	The '*' is a wildcard; will find Test or Test Record but not TEST or New Test
Starts with Text, not case sensitive	@Test*	Will find TEST or TEST RECORD or Test or Test Record but not New Test or greatest
Contains Text anywhere, not case sensitive	@*test*	Combines the @ and the *; will find any record that contains the characters anywhere regardless or case; will find TEST or Test, New Test, TEST RECORD, Testing, tested, but not TESS
Ends with Text, not case sensitive	@*test	Will find test or TEST or greatest but not testing or Tested
Blank or empty Text value	''	Two single quotes (NOT a double quote); will find all records that are blank
Not a blank/empty Text value	<>''	Will find all records that contain any value but are not blank or empty
A specific number	67	Will find records that are equal to 67 specifically, but not -67, or 67.56
One of several specific numbers	67|-68	Will find records that are equal to either 67 or -68, but not any other value
Less than a number	<67	Will find records that are less than 67 only; will find 65, or 66.999, or 0, or -12, but not 67 or 68 or 100
Less than or equal to a number	<=67	Will find records that are less than or equal to 67; will find 65, or 66.999, or 67, or 0, or -12, but not 67.00001, or 68, or 100

Greater than a number	>67	Will find records that are greater than 67 only; will find 68, or 100, but not 67, or 0, or -12
Greater than or equal to a number	>=67	Will find records that are greater than or equal to 67; will find 67, or 68, or 100, but not 66.9, or 0, or -12
Not equal to a number	<>67	Will find records that equal anything other than the number; will find 65, or 0, or 69, or 67.01, or -67, but not 67
Anything between a number and another number	60..67	Will find records that equal anything between and including the range of numbers; will find 60, 62.5, 66.99, 67, but not 59.9 or 67.1 or -62

Important Tip: Filters and Missing Data

Everyone who uses filters has at some point opened up a list or window and seen a list of customers or vendors or other data with many items missing, and felt a panicked "what happened to my data?!?". Remember filters stay on until you turn them off. If you ever feel that some of your data is missing, look at the bottom bar. Do you see the word FILTER?

If you see the word FILTER, you have an active filter. Click Show All or Shift+Ctrl+F7 to release the filter and show all of your data.

Customers: The Basics

Overview

The basic sales functions in Navision include creating a new customer record (customer card), creating and posting a sales invoice, and processing a customer payment (deposit). This section provides step-by-step instructions to show you how to create a customer, enter a sales invoice and process a customer payment / deposit in Dynamics Nav / Navision.

Instructions: Create a New Customer Record

In Navision customer records are kept on customer "cards".

1) Go to Financial Management > Receivables > Customers

2) This will open an existing customer card. Hit F3 for a new, blank customer card

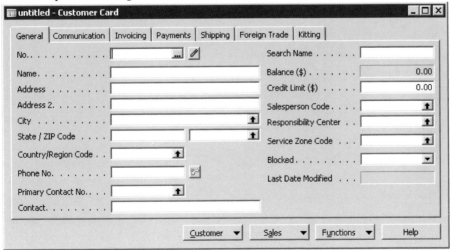

3) Hit the tab key, or click into the Name field, in order to auto-populate the No. field with the next number in the series, or manually type in a number for the new customer record in the number field.

4) Fill in any/all relevant fields with information about the customer. Here are the required fields and why you need them:

To have the customer name and address show up on a customer sales invoice:

   Name (customer/company name, not individual contact name)
   Address
   Address 2 (optional additional line)
   City
   State
   Zip Code

To process any transactions (such as sales invoices or customer payments) for this customer:

Customer Posting Group – pick the appropriate value from the list. Without this value Navision won't know how to connect customer transactions to the appropriate General Ledger account and no transactions involving this customer record will post.

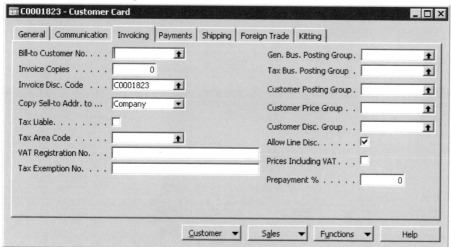

To set the default payment terms for this customer:

Payment Terms Code – Pick an appropriate value (such as Net 30 or COD) for this customer's default payment terms. All newly created sales orders and sales invoices will pull the default payment terms from the customer card.

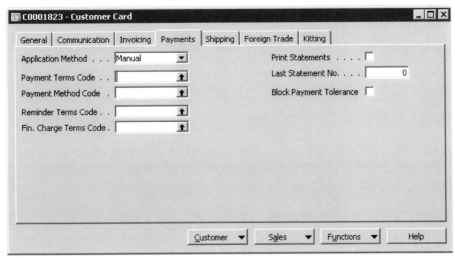

Other fields (such as phone number, email, and so on) may be filled in if desired or if appropriate to your particular business (such as responsibility center or warehouse location).

5) When you have finished filling in the appropriate information for this customer, just hit Escape or click the 'x' to close this card. The information in each field is automatically saved as you tab or click out of that field.

Instructions: Create and Post a Sales Invoice

1) Go to Financial Management > Receivables > Invoices

2) This will open an existing sales invoice if you have unposted sales invoices; otherwise it will open a blank sales invoice. If the invoice you see is not blank, hit F3 to create a new blank sales invoice.

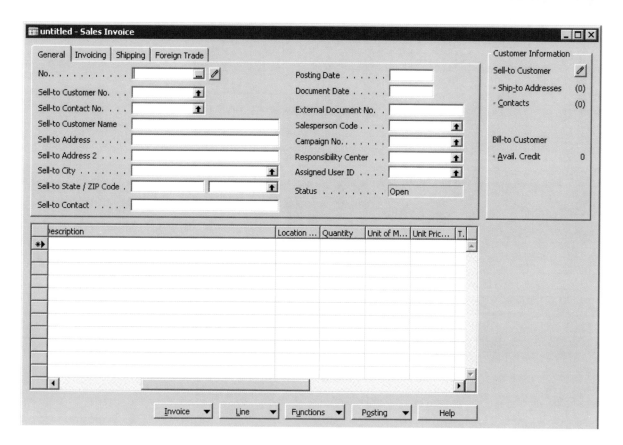

3) Hit tab or click the Sell-to Customer No. field to autopopulate the No. field with the sales invoice number.

4) In the Sell-to Customer No. field, you can enter the customer for this invoice by typing the customer number in directly, or by clicking the arrow or pushing F6 to look up the customer from a list, or by typing in enough of the customer name for Navision to uniquely identify the customer.

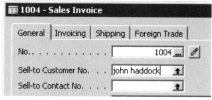

5) Selecting or entering the customer and hitting enter or tab will populate the header (top) section of the sales invoice with information from the customer card, such as name, address, contact, salesperson, terms, and so forth.

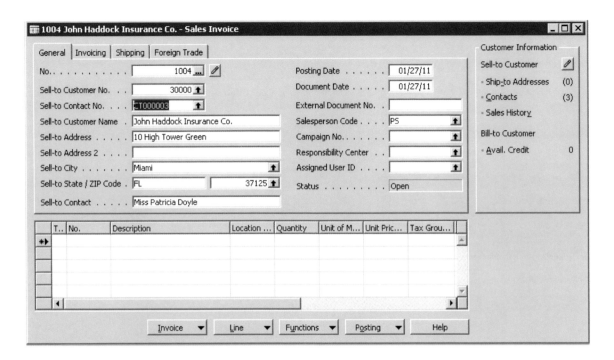

6) The posting date and document date will default to today's date, but you can change them if you want. The posting date is the date the transaction will hit your general ledger and subledgers – so if you are processing an invoice on March 1st but you want it to be "counted" in February's numbers, you need to change the posting date to Feb. 28th. The document date does not impact which fiscal period(s) are affected by a transaction, but it does usually show up on printed invoices, and you can optionally run aging reports based on document date instead of posting date.

7) The customer's payment terms (ie net 30, COD, etc) and whether they are liable for sales tax is set by default from the values on the customer card.

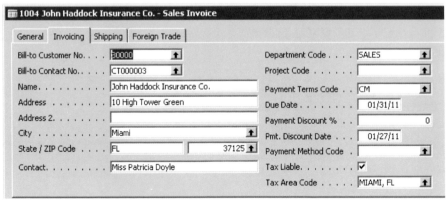

8) Edit or fill in any other fields on the header (top) section that are appropriate for your company and this invoice.

9) Now click on the far left field on the first line on the bottom (lines) section – this is where you enter the information about the products or services for which you are invoicing this customer.

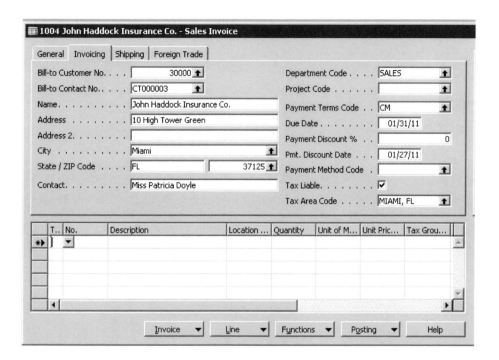

10) From the drop down list, pick the appropriate type of line:

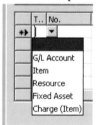

Blank – the blank spot above G/L Account on the list is actually a viable choice – if you pick the blank line, then you can tab over to the description field and enter any notes or comments you want the customer to see at the top of the detail section of their invoice. Using the blank option here makes sure that any comments you type don't confuse Navision into giving you errors when you post.

G/L Account – lets you invoice the customer and have the revenue go direct to the selected General Ledger account. A good choice when the other options such as item, resource or fixed asset do not apply.

Item – lets you invoice the customer for an inventory item. Selecting this option on a sales invoice will allow you to both ship (remove from inventory) and invoice (charge the customer for) an existing inventory item, as long as you are not using the warehouse module of Navision. If you are using the warehouse module, you'll need to first ship the item on a warehouse ship document before you can invoice it. Items are tracked in inventory – you generally need to have bought an item before you can sell it.

Resource – lets you invoice the customer for a resource that has been previously set up in Nav. This is most commonly used for services, such as an hour of someone's time or a day's use of a machine, at a predetermined hourly, daily or per-occurrence rate. Resources are not carried in inventory – you can sell them without buying them first.

Fixed Asset – lets you invoice for a fixed asset that was previously on your company's books as a depreciating asset. This is usually only used when you sell a fixed asset as part of disposing of that asset, ie at the end of it's useful life or when your company no longer needs it. This is not used for selling inventory items that you are in the business of buying and selling routinely.

Charge (Item) – lets you invoice the customer for an extra charge in addition to selling them inventory item(s). These charges are usually things like freight or handling. You can also handle this type of charge as simply a G/L account line going to a freight or handling revenue account, or by setting up a freight resource, but the special advantage of item charges as a line type is that once set up, they automatically go to the correct G/L, and they can spread the revenue associated with the charge across the inventory items proportional to the revenue associated with the items.

11) In the No. field, enter or pick the appropriate account number. Your options in this field are determined based on what you picked in the "account type" field to the left of this field, so if you selected G/L Account, you'll see a list of G/L Account numbers if you click the arrow or hit F6. If you selected Item, you'll see a list of inventory items, Resource and you'll see a list of resources, and so on.

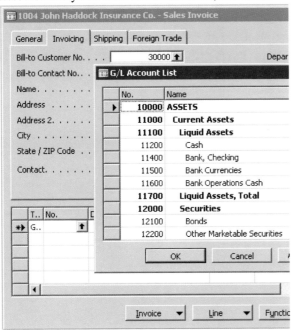

12) Now you simply need to fill in all applicable fields on the line, working left to right. The description will auto-populate from the item number, but you can override it if you want to. The only required/mandatory fields are account type, account number, and quantity. Unit price is not mandatory in a technical sense, but it makes very little sense normally to invoice someone for zero dollars!

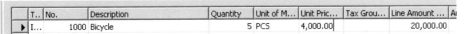

13) The price you will charge your customer is calculated as quantity * unit price = line amount, so in the above example you entered a quantity of 5, and the unit price of $4,000.00 was automatically defaulted from the item

card (although you can change it manually if you want), leading to a line amount before tax of $20,000.

14) Fill in or change any additional fields that are relevant, such as line discount, tax status, etc. When you've finished the first line, tab or down arrow to the start of the next line and fill it in. Add as many lines as you need for this invoice.

15) When you are satisfied that your invoice is complete, you can check your invoice totals by pushing F9 (statistics).

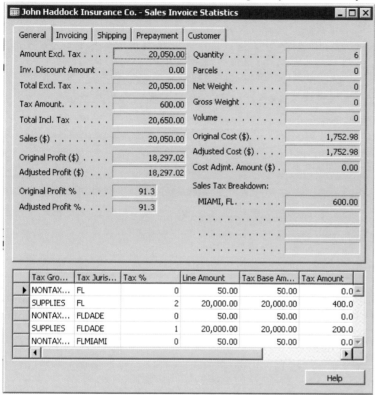

16) This will show you the total invoice amounts with a breakout of sales tax, and various other useful statistics. You can close this window anytime by clicking x or hitting Escape.

17) When you are ready to post, click Posting > Post, or hit F11.

Instructions: Processing a Customer Payment

There are two ways to process customer payments – Deposits and Cash Receipts. This section covers deposits. When you put multiple checks or payment items onto one deposit card in Navision, be aware that each deposit transaction combines all lines to show up on your bank reconciliation as one deposit. So for example if you deposit 5 checks of $100 each on one Navision deposit card, when you do your bank rec you'll see one deposit line for $500, not 5 lines of $100 each.

1) Go to Financial Management > Cash Management > Deposit

2) Hit F3 if needed to get a blank card, then tab or click to auto-generate a deposit number

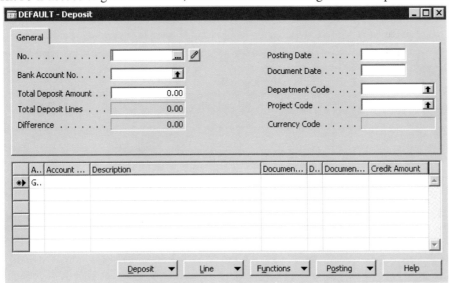

3) Click the up arrow or hit F6 on bank account number to select the bank account where you will deposit the payment(s). Fill out the remaining fields on the header (top) section of the deposit form. Mandatory fields include the posting date (date the deposit will hit your general ledger), document date (can be the same as posting date but does not have to be – some people put the actual date on the deposit slip here), and total deposit amount (this is manually entered and must match the calculated total deposit lines before the system will let you post the deposit.

4) Once the header section is complete, you fill in the lines, one for each deposit item. Required fields are:

Account type – can be any of G/L Account, Customer, Vendor, Bank Account, Fixed Asset, or I/C Partner. As always, which account type you select here will determine which accounts are available in the next field, the No. field. I/C Partner is for intercompany transactions, if you have intercompany set up for your organizations. Customer and Vendor are used for customer payments (the most typical source of deposits), and vendor refunds. Bank Account can be used when the source of the money is the bank, although most companies don't use this option much. G/L Account can be used for misc. payments not attributable to any other source.

Account number – enter or pick from the list the appropriate account number that is the source of your deposit line – most typically this is a customer.

Description – will auto-populate from the account card, but you can edit as you see fit.

Document Date – you should enter the check or payment date here.

Document Type – pick blank, payment or refund. Note that if you pick payment, the account type should be customer – if you pick refund, the account type should be vendor. If you try to set it to an account type of customer and a payment type of refund, for example, you'll get an error when you try to post. Blank is compatible with anything.

Document Number – typically you'd enter the check number here, but you can enter any unique identifier.

Credit Amount – enter the dollar amount of the check or payment here.

5) Once you've finished this line, repeat as needed for as many lines as you have deposit items.

6) You can apply each deposit line to the appropriate sales invoice or purchase credit memo at this time, by clicking Functions > Apply Entries while you are on the line you want to apply.

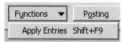

7) When everything is done to your satisfaction, you can post the deposit by clicking Posting > Post or pushing F11.

Vendors: The Basics

Overview

The basic purchase functions in Navision include creating a new vendor record (vendor card), creating and posting a purchase invoice, and making or processing a payment to a vendor ("cutting a check"). This section includes step-by-step instructions to show you how to create a vendor, enter a purchase invoice and make a payment in Dynamics Nav / Navision.

Instructions: Create a New Vendor Record

In Navision vendor records are kept on vendor "cards".

1) Go to Financial Management > Payables > Vendors

2) This will open an existing vendor card. Hit F3 for a new, blank vendor card

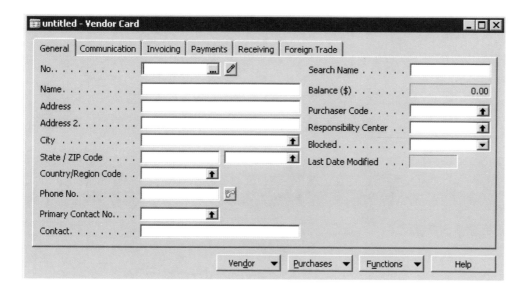

3) Hit the tab key, or click into the Name field, in order to auto-populate the No. field with the next number in the series, or manually type in a number for the new vendor record in the number field.

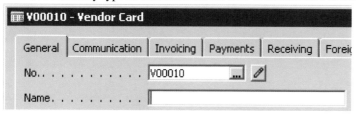

4) Fill in any/all relevant fields with information about the vendor. Here are the required fields and why you need them:

To have the vendor name and address show up on a vendor purchase invoice:

> Name (vendor/company name, not individual contact name)
> Address
> Address 2 (optional additional line)
> City
> State
> Zip Code

To process any transactions (such as purchase invoices or vendor payments) for this vendor:

> Vendor Posting Group – pick the appropriate value from the list. Without this value Navision won't know how to connect vendor transactions to the appropriate General Ledger account and no transactions involving this vendor record will post.

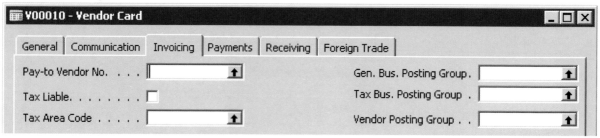

To set the default payment terms for this vendor:

Payment Terms Code – Pick an appropriate value (such as Net 30 or COD) for this vendor's default payment terms. All newly created purchase orders and purchase invoices will pull the default payment terms from the vendor card.

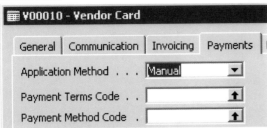

To set the 1099 status and code for this vendor – this is important! If you do not set up 1099 status and codes properly, Navision will let you enter and post transactions, but then when you go to run your 1099 report at the end of the year, you won't see any information! Pick the appropriate 1099 value if applicable, such as MISC-07 for non-employee compensation. Note you must also enter a federal tax ID number for anyone for whom you will be processing 1099's. And, note that "MISC" is not a valid value, you need an extension, like "MISC-07"!

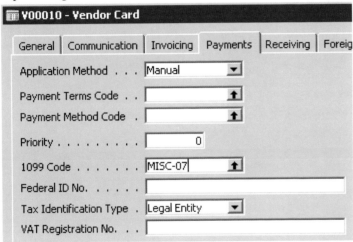

Other fields (such as phone number, email, and so on) may be filled in if desired or if appropriate to your particular business (such as responsibility center or warehouse location).

5) When you have finished filling in the appropriate information for this vendor, just hit Escape or click the 'x' to close this card. The information in each field is automatically saved as you tab or click out of that field.

Instructions: Create and Post a Purchase Invoice

1) Go to Financial Management > Payables > Invoices

2) This will open an existing purchase invoice if you have unposted purchase invoices; otherwise it will open a blank purchase invoice. If the invoice you see is not blank, hit F3 to create a new blank purchase invoice.

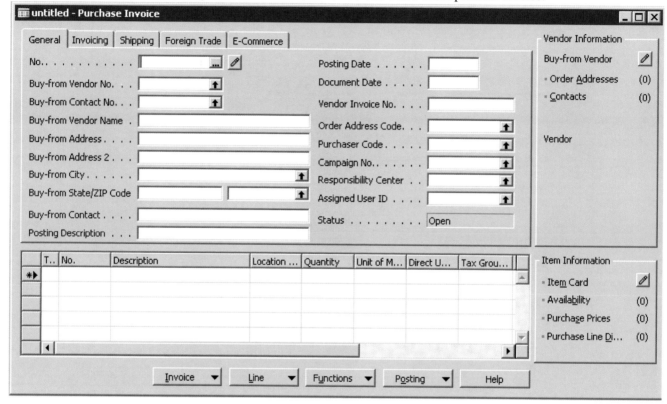

3) Hit tab or click the Sell-to Vendor No. field to autopopulate the No. field with the purchase invoice number.

4) In the Sell-to Vendor No. field, you can enter the vendor for this invoice by typing the vendor number in directly, or by clicking the arrow or pushing F6 to look up the vendor from a list, or by typing in enough of the vendor name for Navision to uniquely identify the vendor.

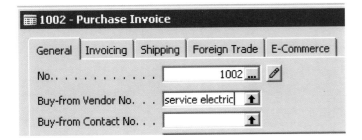

5) Selecting or entering the vendor and hitting enter or tab will populate the header (top) section of the purchase invoice with information from the vendor card, such as name, address, contact, terms, and so forth.

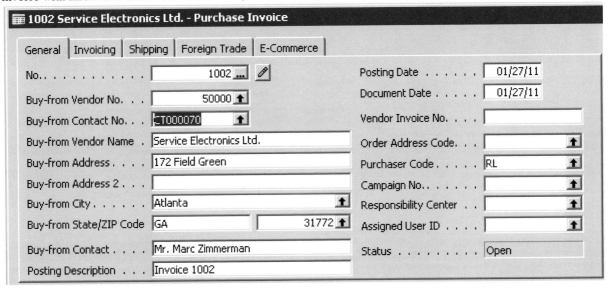

6) The posting date and document date will default to today's date, but you can change them if you want. The posting date is the date the transaction will hit your general ledger and subledgers – so if you are processing an invoice on March 1st but you want it to be "counted" in February's numbers, you need to change the posting date to Feb. 28th or some other data. The document date does not impact which fiscal period(s) are affected by a transaction, but it does usually show up on printed invoices, it is involved in determining when the bill should be paid, and you can optionally run aging reports based on document date instead of posting date.

7) The vendor's payment terms (ie net 30, COD, etc) and whether they are 1099 vendors is set by default from the values on the vendor card.

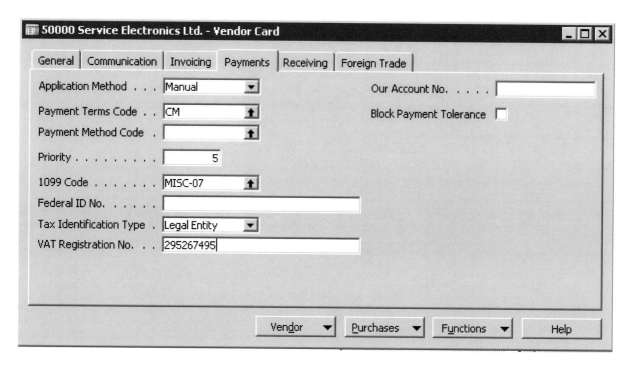

8) Edit or fill in any other fields on the header (top) section that are appropriate for your company and this invoice.

9) Now click on the far left field on the first line on the bottom (lines) section – this is where you enter the information about the products or services which you received from this vendor.

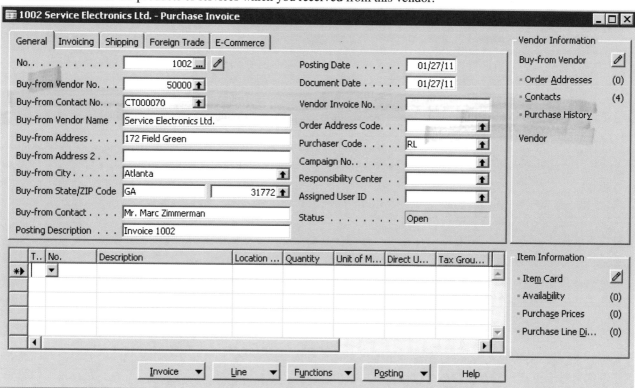

10) From the drop down list, pick the appropriate type of line:

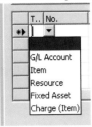

Blank – the blank spot above G/L Account on the list is actually a viable choice – if you pick the blank line, then you can tab over to the description field and enter any notes or comments you want to see at printed at the top of the detail section of the vendor's invoice. Using the blank option here makes sure that any comments you type don't confuse Navision into giving you errors when you post.

G/L Account – lets you process the vendor's invoice such that the costs go directly to the selected General Ledger account. A good choice when the other options such as item, resource or fixed asset do not apply.

Item – lets you process the purchase of an inventory item. Selecting this option on a purchase invoice will allow you to both receive (add to inventory) and invoice (record the purchase cost for) an existing inventory item, as long as you are not using the warehouse module of Navision. If you are using the warehouse module, you'll need to first receive the item on a warehouse receipt document before you can invoice it. Items are tracked in inventory – you generally need to have bought an item before you can sell it.

Resource – lets you process the purchase of a resource that has been previously set up in Nav. This is most commonly used for services, such as an hour of someone's time or a day's use of a machine, at a predetermined hourly, daily or per-occurrence rate. Resources are not carried in inventory – you can buy them without needing to sell or dispose of them later.

Fixed Asset – lets you record the purchase of a fixed asset and put it on your company's books as a depreciating asset. This is only used when you buy a fixed asset that you are keeping to use, it is not used for buying inventory items that you are in the business of buying and selling routinely.

Charge (Item) – lets you record an extra charge from your vendor in addition to the purchase cost of inventory item(s). These charges are usually things like freight or handling. You can also handle this type of charge as simply a G/L account line going to a freight or handling cost account, or by setting up a freight resource, but the special advantage of item charges as a line type is that once set up, they automatically go to the correct G/L, and they can spread the costs associated with the charge across the inventory items proportional to the inventory purchase costs associated with the items.

11) In the No. field, enter or pick the appropriate account number. Your options in this field are determined based on what you picked in the "account type" field to the left of this field, so if you selected G/L Account, you'll see a list of G/L Account numbers if you click the arrow or hit F6. If you selected Item, you'll see a list of inventory items, Resource and you'll see a list of resources, and so on.

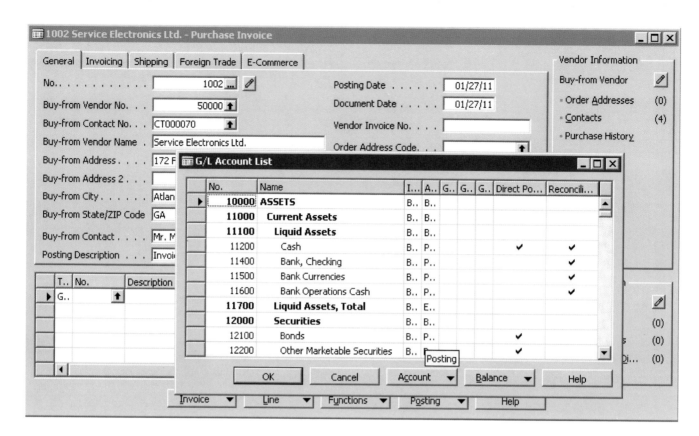

12) Now you simply need to fill in all applicable fields on the line, working left to right. The description will auto-populate from the item number, but you can override it if you want to. The only required/mandatory fields are account type, account number, and quantity. Unit price is not mandatory in a technical sense, but it makes very little sense normally to record an invoice for zero dollars!

	T..	No.	Description	Quantity	Unit of M...	Direct U...	Tax Grou...	Line Amount ...	
▶	I...	1000	Bicycle	3	PCS	500.00	NONTAX...	1,500.00	

13) The price total per line is calculated as quantity * unit price = line amount, so in the above example you entered a quantity of 3, and the unit price of $500.00 was automatically defaulted from the item card (although you can change it manually if you want), leading to a line amount before tax of $1,500.

14) Fill in or change any additional fields that are relevant, such as line discount, tax status, 1099 code, etc. When you've finished the first line, tab or down arrow to the start of the next line and fill it in. Add as many lines as you need for this invoice.

15) When you are satisfied that your invoice is complete, you can check your invoice totals by pushing F9 (statistics).

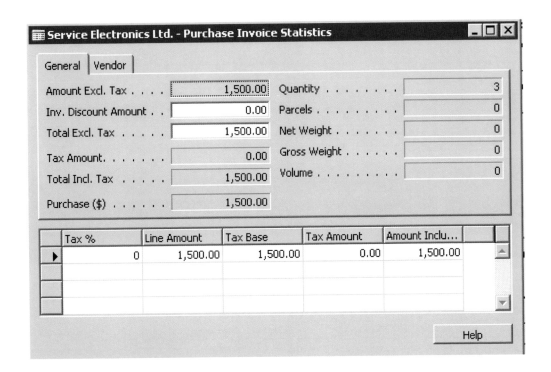

16) This will show you the total invoice amounts with a breakout of discounts, tax, and various other useful statistics. You can close this window anytime by clicking x or hitting Escape.

17) When you are ready to post, click Posting > Post, or hit F11.

Instructions: Processing a Vendor Payment

1) Go to Financial Management > Cash Management > Payment Journal

2) You can get Navision to suggest which vendors and which invoices you should pay by running the suggest vendor payments function.

3) You can set filters to only include certain vendors, or filter by payment method code, or by a range of other fields. Just enter the values you want to filter by on the vendor tab, or leave the right side blank if you want to include all vendors.

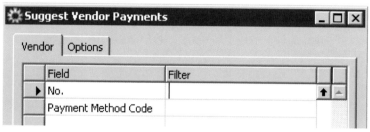

4) If you want to filter on fields not shown, such as vendor posting group, you can click on the left hand "field" column and pick that field from the list, then enter the filtering criteria on the right in the "filter" column.

5) When you have set the filter criteria the way you want, click on the options tab. Many fields here are mandatory and/or important.

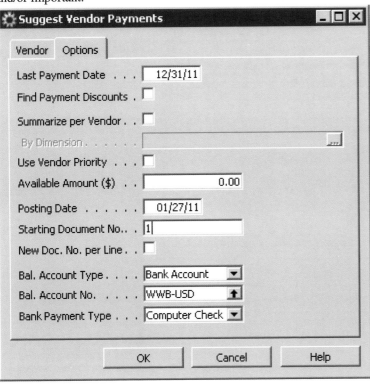

Last Payment Date: The date you put here controls the "pay through" date – meaning, if you want your suggested payments to include everything that is due up through and including the end of the month, put the last day of the month here. If you only want it to show bills due as of today, put today's date here. If you want it to show more or less everything, put a date in the far future here.

Find Payment Discounts: If you check this checkbox, bills that are within the payment discount date will be included even if they are not yet due for their full amount. For example, if your terms with a vendor are 2% 10 net 30, if you check this box, a bill within the 10 day window will be included to be paid. If you leave this checkbox blank, that bill would not be included since it's not yet 30 days.

Summarize Per Vendor: If you check this box, when Navision generates bills to be paid, it will create only one line per vendor, and that line will include the net of all invoices and credit memos within your "pay thru" date. If you leave this box unchecked, it will create a separate line per document.

Use Vendor Priority, and Available Amount: If you check this box, and fill in a dollar amount in the "available amount" field under it, then Navision will only suggest vendor payments up to that dollar amount, and will do so in priority order based on the "vendor priority" field on the vendor card. This is not a commonly used function, and typically this box is left unchecked and the amount field is left blank.

Posting date: The posting date that will be assigned to all suggested payments in this batch. This field must be filled in.

Starting Document No.: This field must be filled in – and it blanks itself out every time you close this window, so you have to re-populate it each time before running suggest vendor payment. You can put your first check number here – or, if you are using computer printed checks and have set them up on the bank card, you can just put a "1" and Nav will automatically pick the correct next check number for you.

New Doc. No. Per Line: If you check this checkbox, Nav will assume you want to issue a separate check for each bill within a vendor – so if you are paying 3 invoices for one vendor, and you check this box, Nav will plan to issue 3 separate checks. If you leave this box blank, Nav will assume you want one check per vendor. For obvious reasons, you cannot check this checkbox and also check the "summarize per vendor" checkbox, and Nav will give you an error if you try.

Bal. Account Type: You can pick from "Bank Account" or "G/L Account". Typically you'll want "bank account", assuming you are paying bills by writing checks or processing electronic payments from your bank.

Bal. Account Number: If you picked "bank account", then you select your specific bank account here. If you picked G/L account, likewise, you select the specific G/L you want to use here.

Bank Payment Type: You can pick from "computer check", "manual check", or "electronic payment" here. If you are going to want Navision to print the checks on a printer, pick computer check. If you are going to hand write or manually create checks, or have already done so, and are simply trying to record this in Nav, pick manual checks. And if you are trying to submit electronic payments (EFTs or ACHs), pick electronic payment.

6) Once you have set all of the options the way you want, click OK

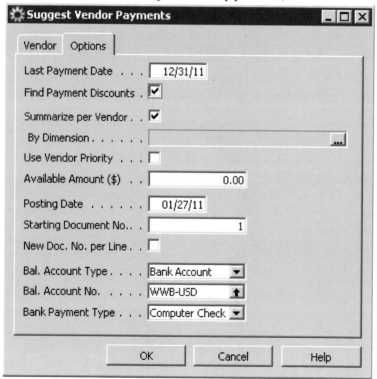

7) Navision will generate a list of vendors and invoices to pay, based on your specifications, and put that list in the Payment Journal.

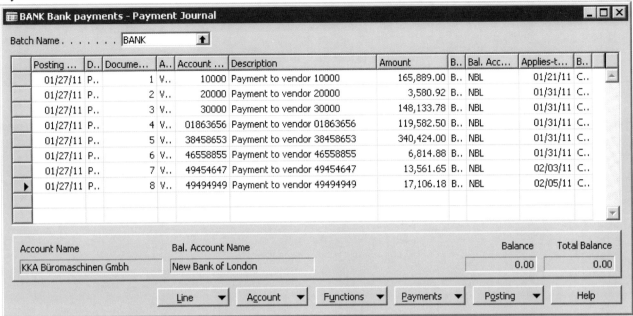

8) Now you can edit the suggested payments if needed, delete any lines you do not want to pay, or make any other changes you wish. You can also manually add payment lines if you need to make a payment that was not suggested by the system. Note that whatever changes you make here only affect the payments that will be made when you post this batch – so if you delete some lines, don't worry, they'll pop right back up next time you run the suggest payments function. You cannot delete invoices here, you can only choose not to pay them.

9) You can also manually add lines in, if you want to make a payment for which you do not have an invoice, or if you simply want to process a payment without using suggest vendor payments, or for some other reason. Just go to a blank line at the bottom, or hit F3 to add a new line.

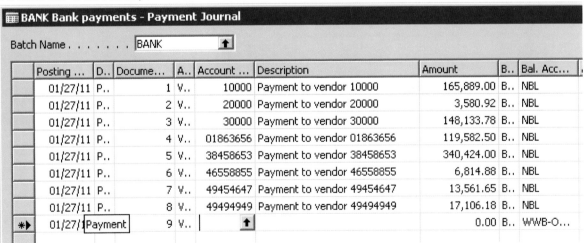

10) If you manually add a lines, you'll need to fill in the posting date, document type (payment), document number (uses the same rules as with automatically generated payments, so just take the next number in the series), account type (usually vendor), select the vendor from the list, and enter the amount. Then make sure the balancing account type is set to bank, the balancing account is set to the bank you want to use to pay these bills, and the bank payment type is appropriately set to computer, manual or electronic.

11) Once your payments are set up the way you want, you can print and review the test report if you like. Go to Posting > Test Report. This step is optional.

12) When you are ready, you can print your checks, if you have selected computer check. To do this, go to Payments > Print Check. If you have selected computer checks, this step is mandatory.

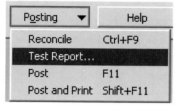

13) On the options tab, make sure that the bank account is properly set to the bank you are using. The last check number should autopopulate, but if it does not, fill it in – remember that Navision will add +1 to this number to get the first check number to use. So in the below example, the first check you print will be #2549.

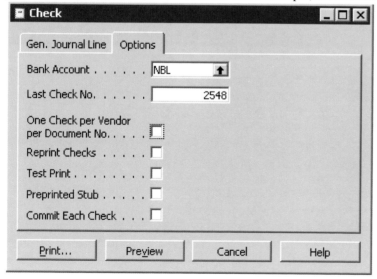

14) The checkboxes are all usually left blank, unless you need their specific function.

The "One check per vendor per document no" should be checked if you want Navision to print a separate check for each vendor/document number combination. This is mostly used if you want to print multiple checks to one vendor in one check run.

"Reprint checks" will make Nav re-use the previously used checks numbers, and let you re-print checks, if you previously printed this batch but for some reason need to re-print.

"Test Print" will print a check format composed of XXXXXXX's. This is used to align your printer, to make sure that your printer will properly print to your checkstock.

"Preprinted Stub" should be checked if your checkstock has preprinted numbers and company name. If this is checked, Nav will not print check numbers, company name, or company address when it prints your checks.

"Commit Each Check" is used to solve certain database sync problems, and should normally be left unchecked.

15) Click Print to print your checks. Once they have printed properly, you are ready to post. Click Posting > Post. Nav will not let you post before you have printed, with computer checks. With manual checks, you skip the printing step and simply post.

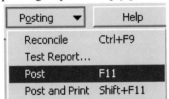

How to Apply a Payment or Credit to an Invoice

Overview

In Navision, it is a good idea to apply payments to invoices in order to close both the payment and the invoice, and to have a record of which payments go with which invoices. Until a payment is applied to an invoice, both the invoice and payment will show as open, which means they will pop up when functions like suggest vendor payment are run. Applying payments to invoices has no General Ledger effect – it does not debit or credit any account, it merely tags the invoices and payments as being connected, and marks them as closed. Credit memos work the same exact way as payments in this regard. This section includes step-by-step instructions to show you how to apply a payment or credit memo to an invoice in Dynamics Nav / Navision.

Instructions: Apply Payment to Invoice in Ledger Entries

1) Go to Financial Management > Payables > Vendors, or Financial Management > Receivables > Customers.

2) This will open a customer or vendor card. Use Ctrl+F on the Name field to search for the customer or vendor for which you want to apply a payment to an invoice. Once you see the customer or vendor you want, push Ctrl+F5 or select Vendor or Customer > Ledger Entries to access the ledger entry detail.

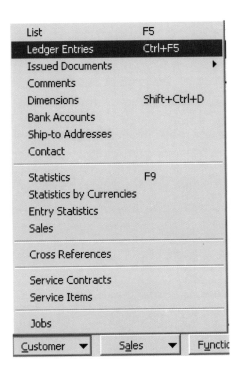

3) You will see a list of all of the posted transactions for this vendor or customer. Find the line with the payment or credit memo you want to apply and click on it.

4) Then push Shift+F9, or click Functions > Apply Entries.

5) The apply entries screen will open up. In the header area, you will see the information on the payment or credit memo you had selected earlier. Click on the line with the invoice you want to apply the payment to.

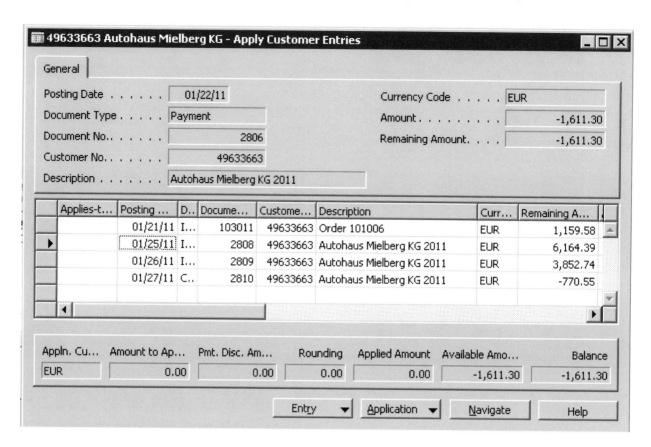

6) Push F9 or select Application > Set Applies-to ID.

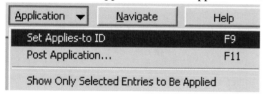

7) This will make an entry show up in the Applies-to column on the Apply Entries screen, and the Amount to Apply field will automatically fill in, but you can edit the amount in the amount to apply field as needed.

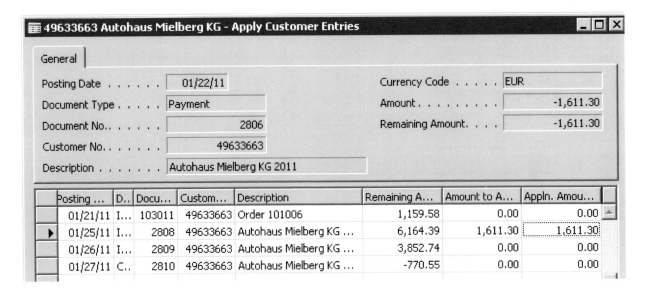

8) You can apply more than one invoice / payment / credit memo at once, just by pushing F9 on each line you wish to apply, but you have to make sure the Balance field shows zero before you can post the application.

9) When you are ready, and the Balance field shows zero, push F11 or Application > Post Application.

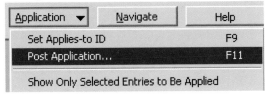

10) You will see a confirmation pop up with the proposed document number and posting date. You can change either of these if you need to, but typically most people don't. Click OK to post the application.

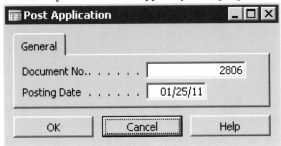

11) You'll see a success message.

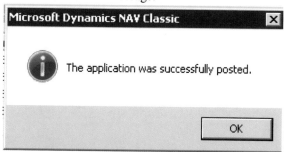

12) If you go back into Ledger Entries, you'll see the payment now shows a remaining amount of zero, and the invoice to which it was applied shows the remaining amount reduced by the payment amount that was applied. Note that the original amounts are unchanged.

Posting ...	D..	Docume...	Custome...	Description	Curr...	Original Amount	Amount	Remaining A...	Due Date
01/21/11	C..	104005	49633663	Credit Memo 104005	EUR	-809.05	-809.05	0.00	01/21/1
01/22/11	P..	2806	49633663	Autohaus Mielberg KG 2011	EUR	-1,611.30	-1,611.30	0.00	02/22/1
01/24/11	P..	2807	49633663	Autohaus Mielberg KG 2011	EUR	809.05	809.05	0.00	02/24/1
01/25/11	I...	2808	49633663	Autohaus Mielberg KG 2011	EUR	6,164.39	6,164.39	4,553.09	02/25/1
01/26/11	I...	2809	49633663	Autohaus Mielberg KG 2011	EUR	3,852.74	3,852.74	3,852.74	02/26/1

How to Delete a Posted Invoice or Credit Memo

Overview

In Navision, if you need to get rid of a posted invoice or posted credit memo, you cannot simply void or delete it. But, there is a simple function called copy document which lets you easily create and post a reversing document to 'cancel out' any invoice or credit memo you wish to eliminate. This section includes step-by-step instructions to show you how to properly reverse a posted invoice or credit memo in Dynamics Nav / Navision.

Instructions: Reverse Posted Invoice

1) Go to Financial Management > Payables > Credit Memos, or Financial Management > Receivables > Credit Memos.

2) This will open a credit memo. If there is already information on it, hit F3 for a new, blank credit memo

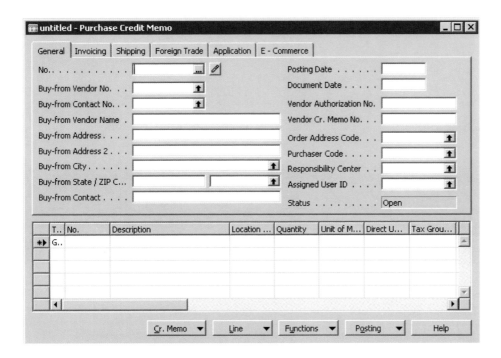

3) Hit the tab key, or click into any field, in order to auto-populate the No. field with the next number in the series, or manually type in a number for the new credit memo in the number field.

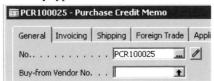

4) Do not fill in any other fields on the credit memo. Instead, go to the Functions button and click Copy Document.

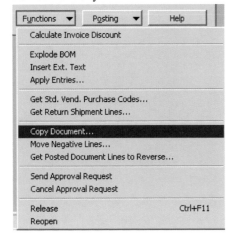

5) The Copy Document screen will open up. For Document Type, select "Posted Invoice". Then click the lookup next to Document No. and select the specific invoice you wish to reverse. Make sure that Include Header is checked (otherwise the header of the resulting credit memo will be blank, which kind of defeats the point). Also

make sure Recalculate Lines is not checked (otherwise it may change values on the invoice lines, which might mean your credit would no longer match your invoice). Click OK.

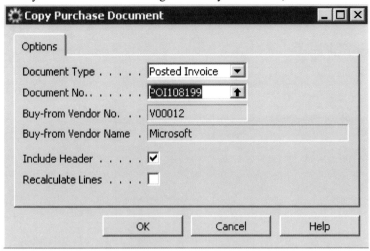

6) Nav will populate the blank credit memo with an exact copy of the data from the purchase invoice, including posting date, document date, lines, amounts, dimensions, tax status – everything.

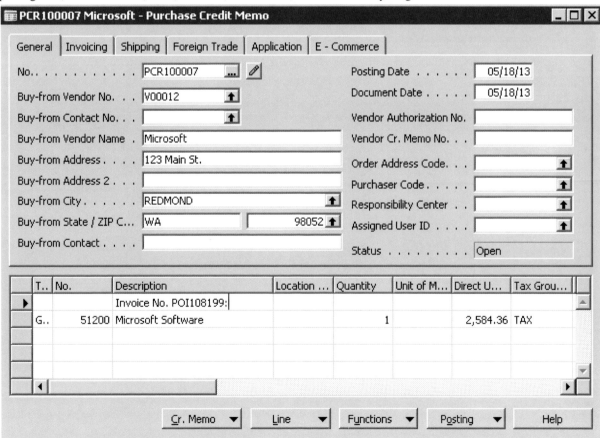

7) The only change is the addition of an information line at the top of the lines section showing which document was

used to generate this copied document – in this case, the number of the posted invoice used in the copy document function. This line has no functional impact, it's just there as a reference.

8) Click Posting > Post, or push F11. Then click Yes to the "Do you want to post" pop up.

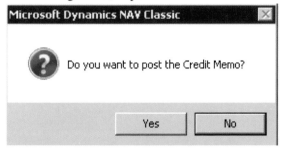

9) The credit memo will post, and will automatically be applied to the invoice. This will effectively cancel out the original invoice and will include reversing entries to the general ledger and all associated subledgers.

Instructions: Reverse Posted Credit Memo

1) Go to Financial Management > Payables > Invoices, or Financial Management > Receivables > Invoices.

2) This will open an invoice. If there is already information on it, hit F3 for a new, blank invoice.

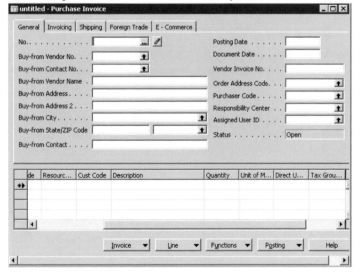

3) Hit the tab key, or click into any field, in order to auto-populate the No. field with the next number in the series, or manually type in a number for the new invoice in the number field.

4) Do not fill in any other fields on the invoice. Instead, go to the Functions button and click Copy Document.

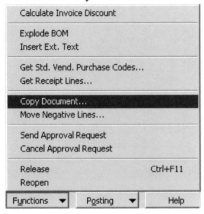

5) The Copy Document screen will open up. For Document Type, select "Posted Credit Memo". Then click the lookup next to Document No. and select the specific credit memo you wish to reverse. Make sure that Include Header is checked (otherwise the header of the resulting invoice will be blank, which kind of defeats the point). Also make sure Recalculate Lines is not checked (otherwise it may change values on the credit memo lines, which might mean your invoice would no longer match your credit memo). Click OK.

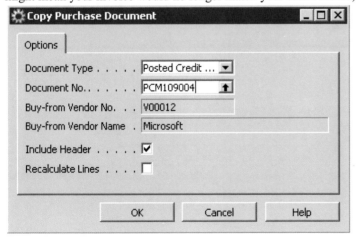

6) Nav will populate the blank invoice with an exact copy of the data from the purchase credit memo, including posting date, document date, lines, amounts, dimensions, tax status – everything.

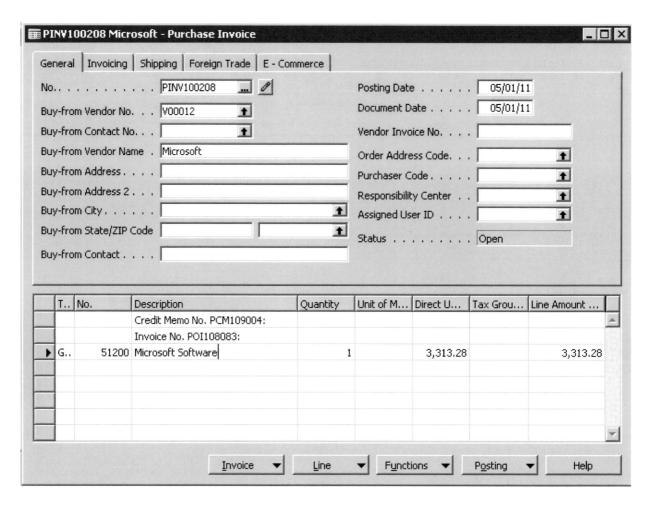

7) The only change is the addition of an information line at the top of the lines section showing which document was used to generate this copied document – in this case, the number of the posted invoice used in the copy document function. Note that if you copy a document that was itself a copied document, you will see two lines, showing the history of each copy, as shown above. These line(s) have no functional impact, they are just there as a reference.

8) Click Posting > Post, or push F11. Then click Yes to the "Do you want to post" pop up.

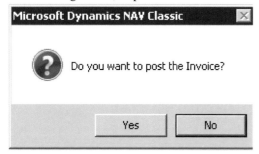

The invoice will post, and will automatically be applied to the credit memo. This will effectively cancel out the original credit memo and will include reversing entries to the general ledger and all associated subledgers.

How to Void a Check

Overview

In Navision, you have three options for voiding checks. You can void a check after it has been printed but not yet posted, or you can void a printed and posted check and reverse it, thus re-opening whatever invoices it paid, or you can void a printed and posted check but leave the invoices it paid closed. Which option you choose depends on your specific needs. This section provides step-by-step instructions to show you how to void a check in Dynamics Nav / Navision.

Instructions: Void a Printed but Not Yet Posted Check

This is useful when you have printed a check but not yet posted it and need to void it – maybe because you've changed your mind about issuing that particular check, or need to issue it in different amount, or from a different bank account. This type of void is basically just an "undo" of the check printing process – there are no GL entries created, because nothing was posted yet, so no GL entries are needed.

1) If you have printed but not posted the check, you will be in the payment journal.

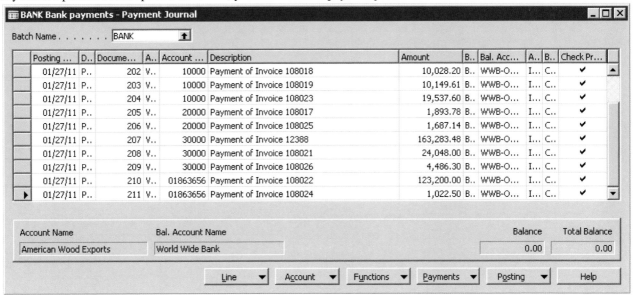

2) If you want to void only one check, put your cursor on the line with the check you want to void, and click Payments > Void Check.

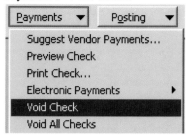

3) You will see a pop up box asking you to confirm that you want to void that check – click Yes.

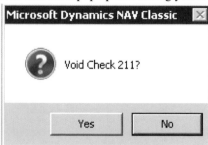

4) Your check is now voided. The other printed checks in this batch are unchanged. You can delete the line and post your batch of properly printed checks – any invoices you were trying to pay will still be there for you to pay next time. Or you can re-do the check printing process for that particular check.

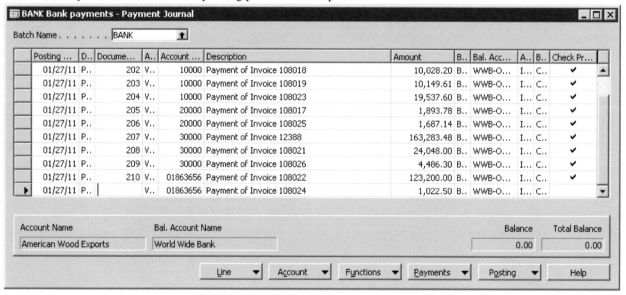

5) If you want to void the entire printed check run all at once, you can instead go to Payments > Void All Checks.

6) You will see a confirmation message – click Yes.

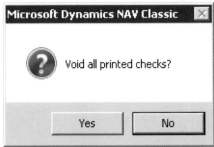

7) All printed checks in your journal are now voided, and you can re-print, or delete and re-run suggest vendor payments to create a new batch.

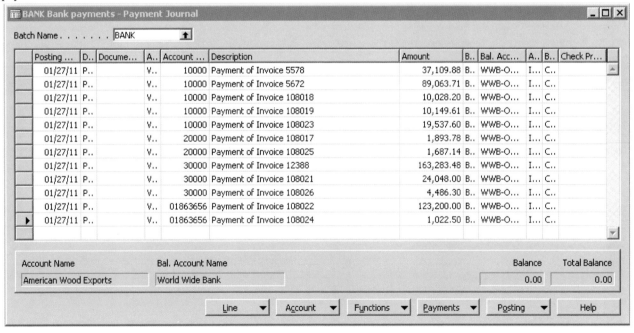

8) Note that with this method of voiding checks, Nav will automatically increment up the last check number on the assumption that you printed physical checks that you had to destroy. However, if for some reason you want to re-use the same check numbers (you forgot to put check stock in the printer and printed on plain paper, for example), you can just change the value in the last check number field next time you print checks. Nav will not stop you from using those numbers again, as long as you never posted them.

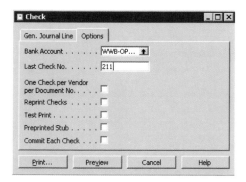

Instructions: Void a Printed and Posted Check

This is useful when you have printed a check but not yet posted it and need to void it

1) Go to the bank card for whichever bank the check was issued from.

2) Select Bank Account > Check Ledger Entries.

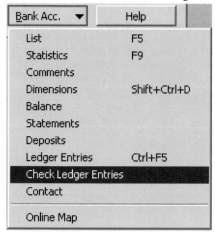

3) Select the check you wish to void. With your cursor on that line, click Check > Void Check

4) You will see the Confirm Financial Void pop up. The Void Date field will be pre-populated with the check date from the check you are voiding, but you can change it if you wish. Note that if you change it, the void transaction may no longer be in the same fiscal period as the original check – but if you leave it alone, and the check was issued some time ago, you may be changing balances for periods you have already closed. You need to make this

decision based on your company's standards and policies for financial reporting.

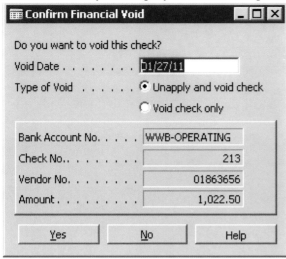

5) If you want to void the check and re-open whatever invoices or entries it was applied to, leave the Type of Void as Unapply and Void Check. This is the most common scenario. It is typically used when for example you have printed a check but then changed your mind and decided not to make that payment, or you need to re-issue the check for a different amount, or with a different check date. If you select this option and click Yes, the check's status will change to Financially Voided.

6) And a new vendor ledger entry will be created showing the voided check cancelling out the payment. The voiding entry will be closed with no remaining amount, but the invoice it paid will now be open again. Note that you cannot re-use this check number.

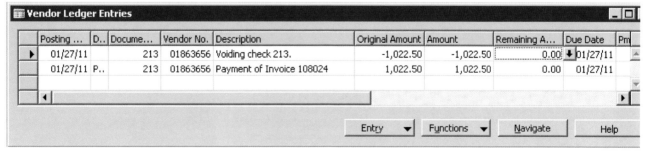

7) Alternatively, if you want to leave the invoices you paid closed but have the voiding entry itself open, you would select Type of Void of Void Check Only. This is done less often, but sometimes is used – for example, if a check

was lost or damaged, and will need to be replaced, but you want to retain the record of paying the invoice with the first check.

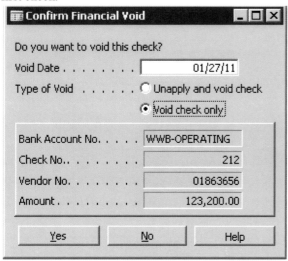

8) This will result in the voided check entry showing an open, unapplied remaining amount, and the invoice that was paid still being closed/paid.

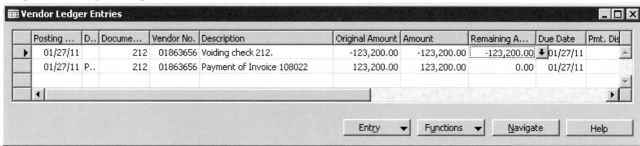

How to Use Prepayments

Overview

The prepayment capability in Navision can be used to process and track prepayments to vendors and/or prepayments from customers. This section provides step-by-step instructions to show you how to use prepayments in Dynamics Nav / Navision, and will cover how to set up and enter prepayments, how to apply the prepayment fully, partially or not at all to subsequent invoices, and how to void or reverse accidental or incorrect prepayments.

Instructions: Create Prepayment Invoice

Prepayments can be created from sales orders or purchase orders. The process is basically the same.

1) Create or open a sales order or purchase order. Fill out the customer/vendor information and the lines showing what will be on the order – this can be anything that would normally go on a sales order or purchase order.

2) Click on the Prepayment tab

3) The fields on the prepayment tab will automatically be pre-populated with standard information such as terms, default prepayment %, etc., from the customer's or vendor's card if you have these set up. Otherwise you'll have to fill them in manually.

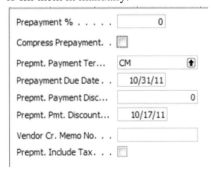

4) If you want your prepayment to apply to the entire invoice, enter the prepayment percentage in the prepayment % field in the header (and then Nav will autopopulate the lines with the same value as per standard Navision behavior). This is the most common situation. If you want the prepayment to only apply to one or more particular lines on the order, leave the header value blank and you'll enter the prepayment amount directly on the line(s).

Direct Uni...	Tax Grou...	Line Amount E...	Prepayment %	Prepmt. Line ...	Prepmt. Amt. ...	(
5,000.00	NONTAX...	5,000.00	0		0.00	0.00

5) Note that the prepayment % field by default will be somewhere to the right of the direct unit cost or price field, but it may not be visible. You may need to use View > Show Column or right click on the columns to un-hide this field before you can use it.

6) On the header or the lines as appropriate, enter the prepayment percentage. Enter it as a whole number – "100" is 100%, "5" is 5%. Do not enter the percent sign, and do not enter a leading decimal. .5 is ½ of one percent, or 0.5%, not 50%.

7) Now – what do you want your prepayment invoice to look like? If your purchase order or sales order has multiple lines, and you want the prepayment invoice to reflect this and show a matching number of lines, then you'll want to make sure that the compress prepayments checkbox on the header is unchecked. Otherwise, (and this is more typical), you can check this box, and your prepayment invoice will have relatively few lines, and typically only one.

8) For example, an order with lines like this:

T...	No.	Description	Quantity	Direct Uni...	Line Amount E...	Prepayment %	Prepmt. Line ...	P
I...	1151	Axle Front Wheel	5,000	0.45	2,250.00	10	225.00	
I...	1110	Rim	800	1.05	840.00	10	84.00	
G..	53350	Delivery Expenses, Raw Mat.	1	50.00	500.00	10	50.00	

9) And the Compress PrePayment box unchecked, with a 10% Prepayment %:

Prepayment % . . . . . [10]

Compress Prepayment. . ☐

10) Will produce a prepayment invoice with the same lines, like this:

Description	Unit	Quantity	Unit Price	Total Price
Axle Front Wheel		1	225.00	225.00
Rim		1	84.00	84.00
Delivery Expenses, Raw Mat.		1	50.00	50.00

11) Whereas the same order with the same lines but with the Compress PrePayment box checked will produce a prepayment invoice with fewer lines and less detail, like this:

Description	Unit	Quantity	Unit Price	Total Price
Vendor Prepayments		1	309.00	309.00
Vendor Prepayments		1	50.00	50.00

12) Next you need to review your prepayment terms. By default, these fields will be populated with values from the vendor / customer card, if available. But you can change these to be anything appropriate, and they also do not have to match the general invoice terms on the invoicing tab. So you can have for example a prepayment invoice with terms of net due on receipt but the terms for the rest of the invoice are 2% 10 net 30.

Prepmt. Payment Ter...	CM
Prepayment Due Date . .	10/31/11
Prepmt. Payment Disc...	0
Prepmt. Pmt. Discount...	10/17/11

13) Once you have the purchase order or sales order prepayment fields on the header and the lines configured the way you want, you general the prepayment invoice by clicking on the Posting button, then Prepayment > Post Prepayment Invoice.

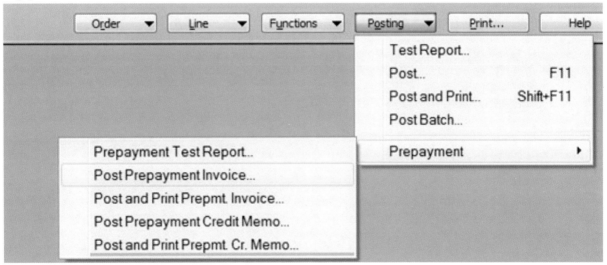

14) You can then review and print this invoice by going to Order > Prepayment Invoices

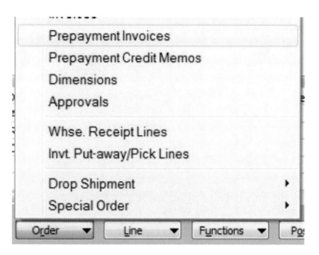

15) You'll see a list of all posted prepayment invoices associated with this order.

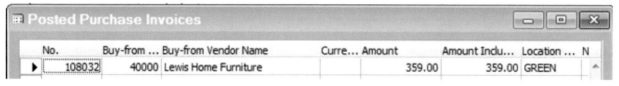

16) And you can then view the invoice by clicking Invoice > Card, or print it directly via the Print button.

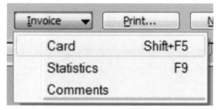

17) You can now pay the purchase prepayment invoice the same as you would any other vendor invoice, or receive payment on a sales prepayment invoice the same way you would any customer payment.

Instructions: Cancel / Void Prepayment Invoice

1) If you processed a prepayment invoice in error, you have to step backwards through the entire process to get rid of it. So, if you created a purchase prepayment invoice and paid it, you first have to void or un-apply the check, so that the invoice is open and unpaid.

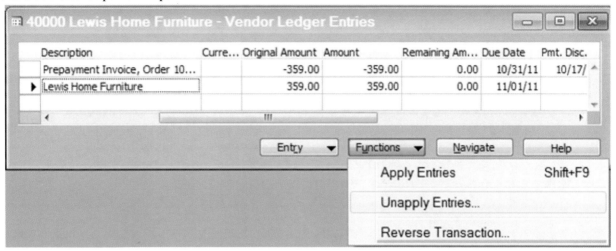

2) Then you have to create a prepayment credit memo from the purchase order or sales order to cancel out the invoice. Note that just making a normal credit memo manually or using the copy document function will not work. Also, note that if your Nav requires external document numbers, for purchase orders you'll need to fill in the vendor credit memo number field on the Prepayment tab of the purchase order before you do the credit memo.

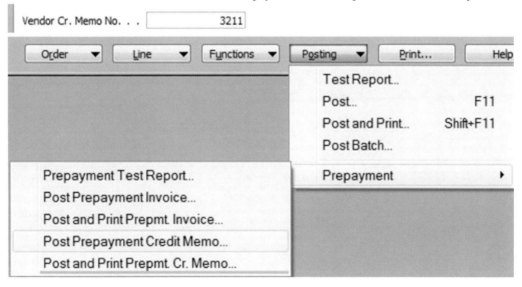

3) Click 'yes' to the confirmation message

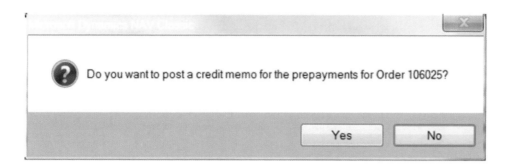

Do you want to post a credit memo for the prepayments for Order 106025?

[Yes]   [No]

4) After you have posted the prepayment credit memo, you will be able to modify or delete the prepayment amount, or otherwise work with the purchase order or sales order as if the prepayment had never happened.

Instructions: Allocating Prepayments on Subsequent Invoices

When you have processed and paid a prepayment invoice against a purchase order, and then you subsequently receive and invoice a purchase order, or ship and invoice a sales order, Navision will by default allocate the prepayment proportionally against the invoice amount.

For example: You have a $500 purchase order.

You make a 10% prepayment of $50.

You receive and invoice ½ of the order, or $250 worth.

Navision will deduct ½ of your prepayment ($25) from the $250 invoice

Leaving you owing the vendor $250 less $25, or $225.

And with the remaining $25 as a pending prepayment.

This is simple enough when you are used to it, but unfortunately it very often does not reflect how real prepayments work in real vendor/customer relationships.

In real life, you may need to deduct the entire prepayment from the very first shipment or receipt and invoice. Or you may need to wait and hold the prepayment against the last invoice. Or possibly some other arrangement.

Fortunately, it's easy to make Navision accommodate to your needs. When you are ready to invoice a PO or SO, do this:

1) Go to your PO or SO. Look on the lines. If the column "Prepmt Amt to Deduct Excl. Tax " is not shown, do View > Show Columns to add it.

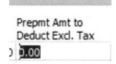

Prepmt Amt to
Deduct Excl. Tax
) 0.00

2) Edit your quantity to invoice field as usual to reflect what you want to invoice. Then look at the amount in the Prepmt Amt to Deduct Excl. Tax field. It will be filled in by default with the proportional amount based on how much you are invoicing.

Qty. to Invoice	Quantity Invoiced	Prepmt Amt to Deduct Excl. Tax	Prepmt Amt Deducted Excl...
200	2,500	9.00	112.50

3) Edit the amount as needed. You can set it to zero if you do not want any of the prepayment used on this invoice. Or you can set it to any amount up to and including the total remaining prepayment amount for that specific line.

Qty. to Invoice	Quantity Invoiced	Prepmt Amt to Deduct Excl. Tax	Prepmt Amt Deducted Excl...
200	2,500	112.50	112.50

4) Repeat this for each line on the purchase order or sales order until it is set up showing the correct prepayment amount to deduct. Then post the document.

How to Set Up Fixed Assets

Overview

Navision has a built-in Fixed Asset system which allows you to maintain a subledger of fixed assets. This subledger can either be integrated with Nav's General Ledger, or kept separate. With Fixed Assets, you can create a card for each asset, track serial numbers, warranties, maintenance agreements, and insurance by asset, categorize assets into classes and subclasses, set up individual depreciation schedules, and much more. This section provides step-by-step instructions to show you how to set up Fixed Assets in Dynamics Nav / Navision.

Instructions: Fixed Asset Setup

1) Fill the Depreciation Book Card

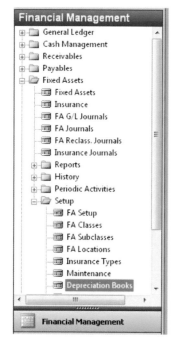

Navigate to Financial Management > Fixed Assets > Setup > Depreciation Books

In this window, you set up the depreciation book or books that must be used for each of the fixed assets. Here you also specify the way depreciation must be calculated. You can set up an unlimited number of depreciation books for a fixed asset, and for each book you can specify individual depreciation terms.

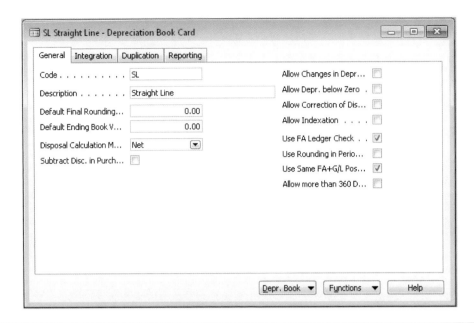

Field name	Description
Code	Enter a name or number to identify the depreciation book.
Description	Short description of the depreciation book. Useful is using more than one depreciation book.
Allow Changes in Depr. Fields	If checked then it is possible to change settings in depreciation book subform located in fixed asset card. If the field is not checked, then no changes are allowed after the first record is posted to current depreciation book.
Allow Depr. below Zero	Place a check mark in this field to allow the Calculate Depreciation batch job to continue calculating depreciation even if the book value of the fixed asset is zero or below.
Use FA Ledger Check	In this field you can indicate which checks you want the program to perform before posting a journal line.

A check mark in the field forces the program to check that:

acquisition cost is the first entry (FA posting date is used).

acquisition cost is entered as a debit.

disposal (if any) is the last entry (FA posting date is used).

depreciable basis has a debit balance. |

	book value has a debit balance unless there is a check mark in the Allow Depr. below Zero field in the depreciation book. accumulated depreciation, accumulated salvage value and accumulated sales price have credit balances. write-down, appreciation, custom 1 and custom 2 entries match the setting in the Sign field in the FA Posting Type Setup window. If this field is blank, the program only checks that: acquisition cost is the first entry (FA posting date is used). disposal (if any) is the last entry (FA posting date is used).
Use same FA+G/L Posting Dates	Place a check mark in this field to indicate that the Posting Date and the FA Posting Date must be the same on a journal line before the line can be posted.

It is also important to mark which entries will be integrated with general ledger. It is done in Integration tab of Depreciation book card.

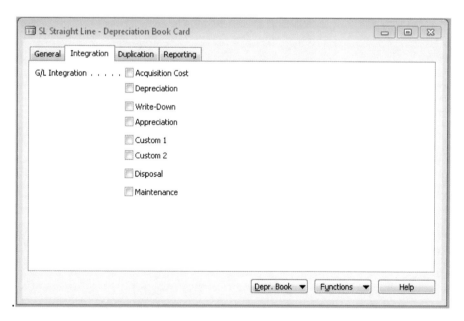

e.g. Place a check mark in this field if you want acquisition cost entries that are posted to this depreciation book to be posted both to the general ledger and the FA ledger. If you have placed a check mark in the field, you must use the FA G/L journal to post acquisition cost entries. If you do not place a check mark in the field, you must use the FA journal to post acquisition cost entries, which will be posted only to the FA ledger.

2) Create FA number series

Before creating FA card, you must create No. Series for the fixed assets.
Navigate to Financial Management > Setup > No. Series

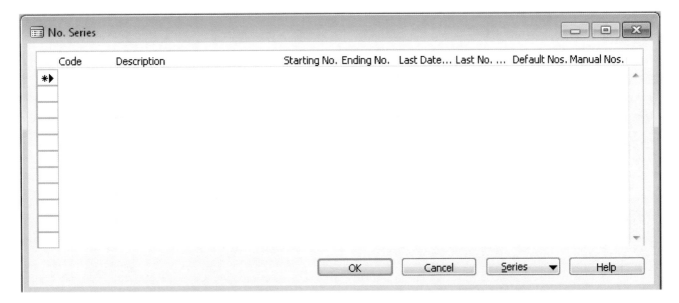

The fields you should fill in are as follows:

Field name	Description
Code	The code for the identification of your No. Series
Starting No.	This field should contain the first number in your number series.
Ending No.	This field could contain the number that should finish your number series.
Last Date	This field displays the date when a number was most recently assigned from the number series. This field is filled in automatically.
Last No.	This field contains the last number that was used from the number series. This field is filled in automatically.
Default Nos.	Here you can indicate whether this number series will be used to assign numbers

	automatically when creating new FA card.
Manual Nos.	A check mark in this field indicates that the program will allow you to enter numbers manually instead of always using this number series.

3) Fill the FA Setup Card

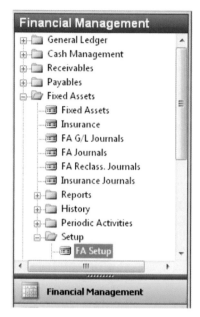

Navigate to Financial Management > Fixed Assets > Setup > FA Setup

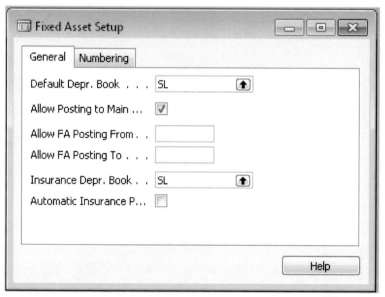

In the Fixed Asset Setup window, you set up certain basic and general information about fixed assets, for example posting period and number series.

Field name	Description
Default Depr. Book	In this field, click the AssistButton, and then select the depreciation book you want the program to suggest as the default book on journal lines, purchase lines and when you run batch jobs and reports.
Allow Posting to Main	Click to enter a check mark in this field if you have split your fixed assets into main assets and components and you want to be able to post directly to main assets. Click to remove the check mark if you only want to allow posting to components.
Allow FA Posting From	Here you can enter the earliest date on which posting to the fixed assets is allowed.
Allow FA Posting To	Here you can enter the latest date on which posting to the fixed assets is allowed.
Insurance Depr. Book	In this field, you can enter one of the depreciation book codes. If you use the insurance facilities, you must enter a code in order to be able to post insurance coverage ledger entries. The program uses the code in this field when it automatically disconnects sold fixed assets from insurance policies. Click the AssistButton in the field, and then select a code. To ensure full disconnection of sold assets, select a depreciation book code that has been assigned to all fixed assets.
Automatic Insurance Posting	A check mark in this field tells the program to post insurance coverage ledger entries automatically when you post acquisition cost entries with the Insurance No. field filled in. No check mark in this field, means the program creates lines in the insurance journal instead of posting to the insurance coverage ledger entries.

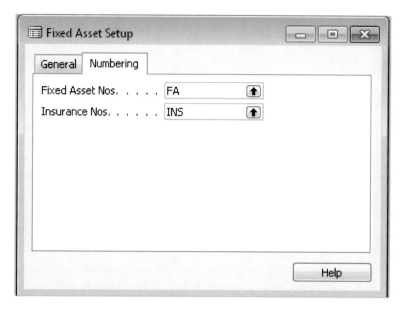

Field name	Description
Fixed Asset Nos.	Here you can enter the code for the number series that will be used to assign numbers to fixed assets.
Insurance Nos.	Here you can enter the code for the number series that will be used to assign numbers to insurance policies.

4) Fill in the FA Posting Groups

Navigate to Financial Management > Setup > Posting Groups > Fixed Asset

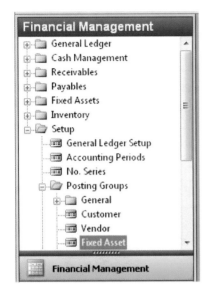

In the FA Posting Groups window, you specify for each posting group the accounts to which the program will post transactions involving fixed assets. After you have set up the posting groups, you assign them to the relevant fixed assets.

In the following situations, the program will then use the information represented by the code to post to the accounts you specified:

Posting of purchase orders, invoices or credit memos
Posting of fixed asset transactions using journals
Posting journals with the help of the Calculate Depreciation batch job
Posting journals with the help of the Index Fixed Assets batch job
Posting groups also let you group fixed assets for statistical purposes.

Field name	Description
Code	Enter the name of the asset type.

Acquisition Cost Account	Enter the G/L account number to which acquisition costs will be posted.
Accum. Depreciation Account	Enter the G/L account number to which depreciation will be posted.
Acq. Cost Acc. on Disposal	Enter the G/L account number to which acquisition costs will be posted when the asset is sold.
Accum. Depr. Acc. on Disposal	Enter the G/L account number to which depreciation will be posted when the asset is sold.
Gains Acc. on Disposal	Enter the G/L account number to which gain will be posted when the asset is sold.
Losses Acc. on Disposal	Enter the G/L account number to which losses will be posted when the asset is sold.
Maintenance Expenses Account	Enter the G/L account number to which maintenance costs will be posted.
Depreciation Expenses Account	Enter the G/L account number to which depreciation will be posted (debit).

5) Fill in FA Classes

Navigate to Financial Management > Fixed Assets > Setup > FA Classes

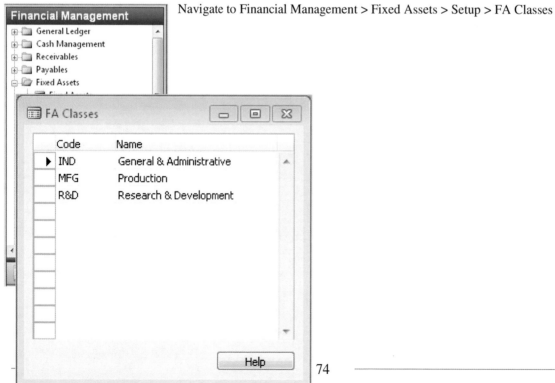

You use the FA Classes window to set up asset classes (for example, tangible and intangible assets) in order to group your fixed assets by categories. After the FA class codes have been set up, you can assign them to fixed assets and insurance policies.

6)   Fill in FA Subclasses

Navigate to Financial Management > Fixed Assets > Setup > FA Subclasses

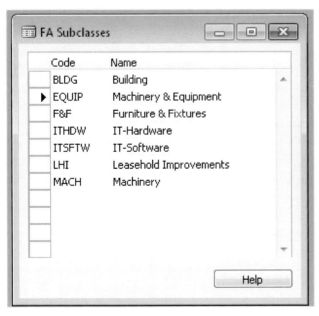

You can use the FA Subclasses window to set up asset subclasses, for example, plant and property, and machinery and equipment. After the FA subclass codes have been set up, you can assign them to fixed assets and insurance policies.

Creating Fixed Asset Card

When you set up a new fixed asset, there are fields that must always be filled in, fields that can be filled in as needed and fields in which you cannot enter anything. The checklist below shows the fields on each tab in the standard layout.

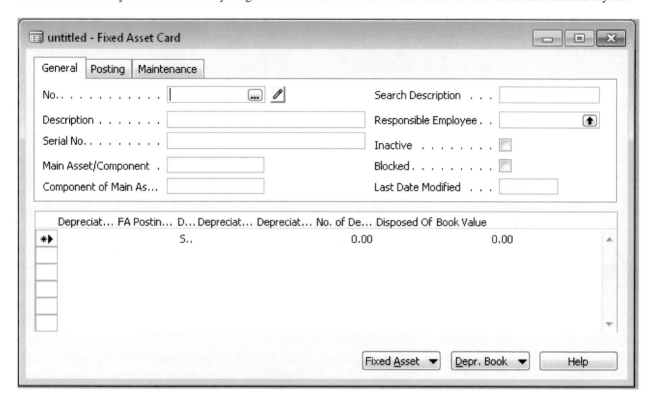

Field name	Description	Fill in
No.	Enter a unique number. If automatic numbering is activated, just press enter in this field to get the next available number.	Must be filled in.
Description	Enter description of fixed asset	Can be filled in
Serial No.	Enter a unique identification number assigned to the asset. This number will help you track the asset if you own several	Can be filled in

	similar items (for example, several personal computers)	
Main Asset/Component	When a component list has been set up, the program fills in Main Asset or Component.	Filled in automatically.
Component of Main Asset	If the fixed asset is a component of another asset, the program fills in the number of the main asset.	Filled in automatically
Search Description	The fixed asset description is assigned as a default, but it can be changed.	Can be filled in.
Responsible Employee	Click the AssistButton to see the list of employees. Select a person and click Ok.	Can be filled in.
Inactive	Check if you want to deactivate a fixed asset. Inactive assets are omitted in batch jobs and reports and blocked from posting	Can be filled in.
Blocked	Check if you want to block posting to fixed asset. Blocked assets are omitted in batch jobs which create journal lines.	Can be filled in.
Last Date Modified	The program automatically fills in the date of the last change of information on the account.	Filled in automatically.
Posting Tab		
FA Class Code	Click the AssistButton to see the list of FA classes. Select relevant code, and then click Ok.	Can be filled in.
FA Subclass Code	Click the AssistButton to see the list of FA subclasses. Select relevant code, and then click Ok.	Can be filled in.
FA Location Code	Click the AssistButton to see the list of FA locations. Select relevant code, and then click Ok.	Can be filled in.
Budgeted Asset	Check if the asset is a budgeted asset. Budgeted assets cannot have G/L integration.	Can be filled in.
Department Code	Click the AssistButton to see the list of departments. You can use this field to	Can be filled in.

	specify to which department the asset belongs. This can be useful when you look at financial information, broken by departments, elsewhere in the program. Select the relevant code, and then click Ok.	
Project Code	Click the AssistButton to see the list to projects. Select the relevant code, and then click Ok.	Can be filled in.
Maintenance tab		
Vendor No	Enter the number of the vendor that supplied the fixed asset.	Can be filled in.
Maintenance Vendor No	Enter the number of the vendor who usually performs maintenance on the fixed asset.	Can be filled in.
Under Maintenance	Check if the asset is under maintenance. You can then filter various reports in order to see which assets are under maintenance.	Can be filled in.
Next Service Date	Enter the date of the next scheduled service. The field is used as a filter in the Maintenance – Next Service report.	Can be filled in.
Warranty Date	Enter the warranty expiration date. This is for information purposes only.	Can be filled in.
Insured	The program automatically checks it if the asset is covered by an insurance policy.	Filled in automatically.

You can use various depreciation methods for your fixed assets. If you want to be able to depreciate one or more fixed assets by several depreciation methods, you must set up multiple FA depreciation books.

After you have set up the necessary depreciation books, you must attach one or more books to each fixed asset. You do this by creating FA depreciation books. For each FA depreciation book you create, you must specify the depreciation method and some other information. FA depreciation books are created using a subform in FA card form.

The following fields must be filled in:

Field name	Description
Depreciation Book Code	In this field fill in one of the depreciation

	books you have set up to assign it to the fixed asset you have entered in the FA No. field.
FA Posting Group	In this field, enter the FA posting group that must be used when posting entries to the current depreciation book. The account for depreciation calculation must be filled in with the chosen FA posting group.
Depreciation Method	Here you can select the method the program must use when calculating depreciation in the current depreciation book for the current fixed asset.
Depreciation Start Date	Here you must enter the date on which you want the depreciation calculation to start.
Depreciation End Date	Here you can enter a date to specify the length of the depreciation period. You must have filled in the Depreciation Starting Date field before you can fill in this field.
No. of Depreciation Years	Here you can enter the length of the depreciation period, expressed in years. You must have filled in the Depreciation Starting Date field before you can fill in this field.

When you enter a number in this field, the program automatically fills in the Depreciation Ending Date. |

The Disposed Of field contains a check mark if the fixed asset has been disposed of.

The program calculates the contents of the field using the entries in the FA Ledger Entries window. Those entries with Yes in the Part of Book Value field are added and shown in the Book Value field.

Posting to the FA G/L journal

There are two types of FA journals – the FA journal and FA G/L journal. FA G/L journal is integrated with General Ledger (the information posted also goes to General Ledger) and is used for operations like FA Acquisition, FA Depreciation or FA Disposal. Meanwhile, information posted into FA journal stays only there.

To post FA Acquisition navigate to:
Financial Management > Fixed Assets > FA G/L Journals

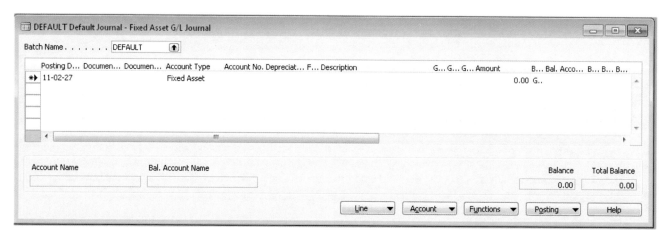

On the FA G/L journal the following fields must be filled in:

Posting Date – the date of the entry being posted.

Document No. – the document no. must be specified here. However, if journal batch contains the number series code, this field is filled in automatically.

Account Type – the account type is automatically filled in as Fixed Asset.

Account No. – here you must specify the fixed asset you will be using.

Depreciation Book – here depreciation book must specified from the depreciation books you have created.

FA Posting Type – here is the type of the posting entry specified. For the acquisition of a fixed asset you should pick Acquisition Cost.

Amount – the amount a fixed asset is being acquisitioning for.

Bal. Account Type – the balancing account type that should be used in the journal line. This field is automatically filled with G/L Account.

Bal. Account No. - the number of the G/L, customer, vendor or bank account to which a balancing entry for the journal line will posted (for example, a cash account for cash purchases).

After filling in these fields and all the required dimensions press F11 for the posting of your entry.

Calculating depreciation

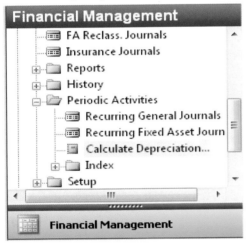

Once a month, or whenever you choose, you can run the Calculate Depreciation batch job. Assets that have been sold, assets that are blocked or inactive on the fixed asset card and assets using the manual depreciation method are ignored.

Navigate to Fixed Assets > Periodic Activities > Calculate Depreciation.

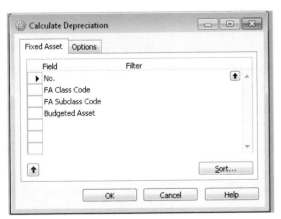

On the Fixed Asset tab you can set filters to select the assets you want to depreciate.

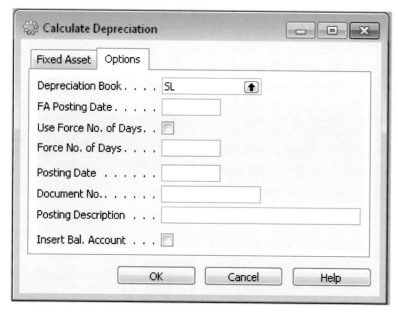

On the Options tab you must pick Depreciation book you will be using.

FA Posting Date must also be filled in as it is the day on which the depreciation is being calculated.

Document No. must be filled in if the journal batch used does not have a number series in the No. Series field. Otherwise it will use the next available number.

Fields Use Force No. of Days and Force No. of Days are always used together and are useful if you want the program to use your given number as a No. of Depreciation Days.

Insert Bal. Account checkbox should be checked you want the batch job to automatically insert balancing accounts in the resulting journal. The batch job uses the accounts you defined in the FA Posting Group table in the Accum. Depreciation Account field.

After running the batch job you should navigate to your FA G/L Journal, review the lines created and press F-11 to post them.

How to Set Up Sales Tax

Overview

How to set up Sales Tax rates for different tax periods and tax jurisdictions, including state, county, city, and other municipality sales taxes. How to set default sales tax liability rules for customers. How to process a Sales Invoice where some lines / items / charges are subject to sales tax and others are not. This section includes step-by-step instructions to show you how to set up United States sales tax in Dynamics Nav / Navision.

Instructions: Sales Tax Setup

1) This is the initial sales tax setup for Navision as a whole. Except as otherwise specified, this will only need to be done once.

2) Navigate to Financial Management > Setup > Sales Tax > Tax Groups.

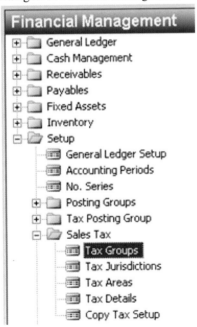

3) Open Tax Groups and add your tax groups. Most organizations will only need two – a taxable group, and a non-taxable group. You can name them whatever you'd like, we use NONTAX and TAX.

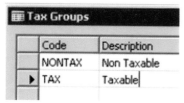

4) Navigate to Financial Management > Setup > Sales Tax > Tax Jurisdictions

5) Fill out the Tax Jurisdiction list. You'll need one entry for each tax jurisdiction. Typically, you'll have one entry for your state, for example Ohio, then another entry for your county or city within that state, for example Cincinnati. Sometimes you'll have a third level, a town or city inside a county, which is inside a state. You then repeat this for each of the different states, counties, cities, or other regions in which you are required to collect and report sales tax. For each line, populate the fields as follows:

Code – Enter any code you want to uniquely identify this tax jurisdiction. We typically use the two-letter state abbreviation for the state, and the state abbreviation followed by a city or county abbreviation for localities within the state, but you can use any system you find helpful as long as each code is unique and no more than 20 characters.

Description – Enter a description of the tax jurisdiction. You may enter anything you like, a plain, clear description is usually best.

Tax Account (Sales) – Enter or push F6 to select the G/L account you want sales tax charges on your customer sales transactions to go to. This is typically a liability account.

Tax Account (Purchases) – Enter or push F6 to select the G/L account to which you want sales tax charged on your purchases to go. This is typically an expense account.

Reverse Charge (Purchases) – Enter or push F6 to select the G/L account to which you want sales tax credited when a purchase is refunded to go. This is typically an expense account, and often the same account as that used in Tax Account (Purchases).

Report-To Jurisdiction – Enter or push F6 to select the Tax Jurisdiction to which you report sales taxes for this Jurisdiction. States typically report to themselves, ie the Report-to Jurisdiction for OH is OH. Counties, cities, and similar localities typically report to the state in which they are located.

Country – Select US or Canada.

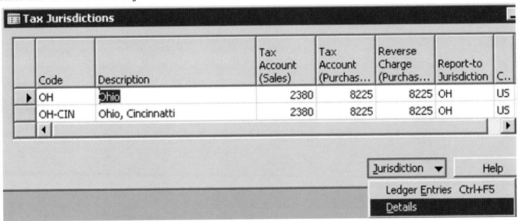

6) For each Tax Jurisdiction, click on the line, then click on Jurisdiction > Details to open the screen where you can enter the tax rates for that jurisdiction.

7) In the Tax Details screen, fill in the fields as follows:

Tax Jurisdiction – Will be pre-populated with the tax jurisdiction you were on when you clicked Details. Don't change it.

Tax Group Code – From the tax group codes you set up earlier, pick the appropriate code. Typically this will be "TAX" or whatever you named your taxable or tax-liable group.

Tax Type – Select Sales Tax or Excise Tax, since you are setting up sales tax, this should be Sales Tax

Effective Date – the date this particular tax rate for this Jurisdiction went into effect. Many tax municipalities change tax rates every year, or month, or quarter. As the rates change, enter new rates on a separate line, with the appropriate start date, and Navision will select the correct tax rate based on your document's dates compared with the start dates of the various taxes.

Tax Below Maximum – Enter the tax rate for your Jurisdiction here. If there's a multi-tier tax rate system in place, enter the tax below the maximum (for example, 3% up to $500, then 5%, you would enter 3.00). If it is a single-tier system, ie Ohio is 5.5%, simply enter that percentage, as a decimal number.

Maximum Amount/Qty – If the Jurisdiction has a multi-tier system, enter the maximum amount here as a decimal number (ie 500.00 in the above example). Leave at zero if this does not apply.

Tax Above Maximum – If the Jurisdiction has a multi-tier system, enter the tax rate once the maximum has been met or exceeded (ie 5.00 in the above example). Leave at zero if this does not apply, in which case the Tax Below Maximum will be used for all transactions.

Expense/Capitalize – Should these tax amounts be expensed or capitalized – does not apply to Sales Tax in most cases, so leave unchecked.

OH Ohio - Tax Details

	Tax Jurisdicti...	Tax Group Code	T.. T..	Effective Date	Tax Below Maximum	Maximum Amount/Qty.	Tax Above Maximum	Expense/...
▶	OH	TAX	S..	01/01/10	5.50	0.00	0.00	

8) Repeat this process to fill out Tax Details for all Tax Jurisdictions. NOTE: Tax for states vs localities should be entered separately. So for example, Cincinnati has a sales tax rate of 6.5% -- 5.5% from the state of Ohio, and 1% from the county of Hamilton. So you'd set up Ohio as a Jurisdiction, with at Tax Below Maximum of 5.50, and also set up Hamilton County, Ohio as a Jurisdiction, with a Tax Below Maximum of 1.00. If Cincinnati has a separate city tax in addition to the state and county taxes, you'd set that up as yet another Jurisdiction, with it's incremental tax rate.

9) Add a line to Tax Details for NONTAX (or whatever you set your nontaxable Tax Group to be). Set the tax rates to zero for this line. NOTE: You must set up the zero-rate non-tax for each Jurisdiction, or you will not be able to set specific invoice lines on the Sales Invoice to non-taxable.

OH Ohio - Tax Details

	Tax Jurisdicti...	Tax Group Code	T.. T..	Effective Date	Tax Below Maximum	Maximum Amount/Qty.	Tax Above Maximum	Expense/...
	OH	NONTAX	S..	01/01/80	0.00	0.00	0.00	
▶	OH	↑ TAX	S..	01/01/10	5.50	0.00	0.00	

10) Navigate to Financial Management > Setup > Sales Tax > Tax Areas.

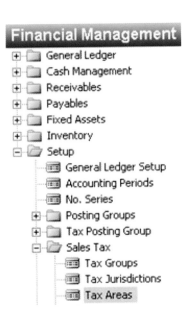

Financial Management

- ⊞ General Ledger
- ⊞ Cash Management
- ⊞ Receivables
- ⊞ Payables
- ⊞ Fixed Assets
- ⊞ Inventory
- ⊟ Setup
  - General Ledger Setup
  - Accounting Periods
  - No. Series
  - ⊞ Posting Groups
  - ⊞ Tax Posting Group
  - ⊟ Sales Tax
    - Tax Groups
    - Tax Jurisdictions
    - **Tax Areas**

11) Using the Tax Jurisdictions you've just entered, set up the Tax Areas. Each Tax Area is a combination of all of the applicable taxes for a particular area. For example, in Cincinnati, Hamilton County, OH is a tax area, which includes the state tax of OH, and the local county tax of OH-HAM for Hamilton County. The Tax Area "rolls up" different taxes that all apply to a given area, and it is Tax Area that you pick to set the sales tax rates when you are calculating an invoice. Fill out the Tax Area card fields as follows:

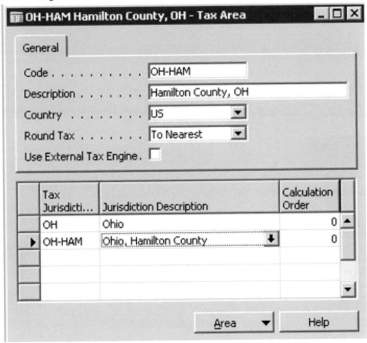

Code – Enter any code that is unique and meaningful to you to identify this unique tax area. We like to use the state, then a dash, then an abbreviation for the county or city, but you can choose whatever suits you. Must be 20 characters or less.

Description -- Enter a description of the Tax Area. You may enter anything you like, a plain, clear description is usually best.

Country – Select US or Canada.

Round Tax – Select the rounding method – To Nearest, Up or Down. To Nearest rounds the traditional way, .5+ rounds up, <.5 rounds down. To Nearest is the usual choice.

Use External Tax Engine – If you are integrated with an external tax calculation engine, check this box. If you don't know what this is, it doesn't apply to you, so leave it unchecked.

Tax Jurisdiction (Lines) – Add all applicable Tax Jurisdictions, one at a time, by selecting from the Tax Jurisdiction field list.

Calculation Order (Lines) – If you need the taxes to be applied or calculated in a particular order, enter it here. Otherwise leave at zero (this is typical).

12) Congratulations! Your Sales Tax Setup is now complete. However, before you can use it, you'll also need to understand how to set up and manage Sales Tax Liability on Customers and/or Sales Invoices.

Instructions: Set Default Sales Tax on Customer Cards

1) You can set up on your customer cards which customers are liable for sales tax, and in which jurisdictions. You can then change or override this on each sales invoice.

2) Open a customer card. Click on the Invoicing tab. To make a customer liable for sales tax, check the Tax Liable checkbox. Then in the Tax Area Code field, push F6 or click the arrow to select the Tax Area Code that will by default apply for this customer.

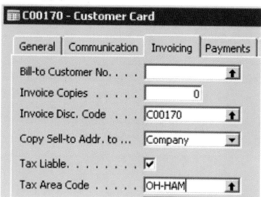

Instructions: Set Sales Tax on Sales Invoices

1) When you create a sales invoice, it will set the Tax Liable and Tax Area Codes for that invoice to whatever you'd specified for that customer on the Customer Card. You can leave it as-is, or change it on an invoice by invoice basis. To change it for a specific invoice, do this:

2) In the Sales Invoice header, click on the Invoicing tab. To have sales tax charged on this invoice, on any invoice line or item, check the Tax Liable box and select the appropriate Tax Area Code from the list. To have no sales tax charged anywhere on this invoice, clear / uncheck the Tax Liable checkbox.

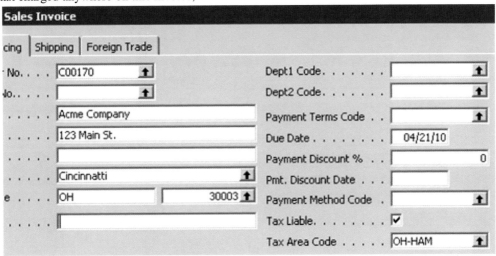

3) You can set each line on the sales invoice separately to be taxable or non-taxable. It will default to the settings you specified in the header, but for any given line, you can specify whether or not to charge tax on that line by setting the Tax Group Code to TAX or NONTAX (or whatever you specified when you set it up). If you set Tax Group Code to NONTAX for a given line, no sales tax will be calculated or charged on that line. NOTE: You cannot uncheck Tax Liable on the lines, but if the Tax Group Code is set to NONTAX, no tax will be charged for that line.

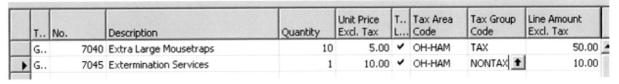

4) You can check to see that tax was calculated correctly on this invoice by pushing F9 and looking at the tax breakdown on the Invoice Statistics screen.

Sales Invoice Statistics

| General | Invoicing | Shipping | Prepayment | Customer |

Amount Excl. Tax	60.00	Quantity	11
Inv. Discount Amount . .	0.00	Parcels	0
Total Excl. Tax	60.00	Net Weight	0
Tax Amount.	3.25	Gross Weight	0
Total Incl. Tax	63.25	Volume	0
Sales ($)	60.00	Original Cost ($).	0.00
Original Profit ($)	60.00	Adjusted Cost ($)	0.00
Adjusted Profit ($) . . .	60.00	Cost Adjmt. Amount ($) .	0.00
Original Profit %	100.0		
Adjusted Profit %	100.0		

Sales Tax Breakdown:

Hamilton County, OH .	3.25
. . . .	
. . . .	
. . . .	

Tax Group Code	Tax Jurisdicti...	Tax %	Line Amount	Tax Base Amount	Tax Amount	Amount Including Tax	
▶ NON... ↑	OH	0	10.00	10.00	0.00	10.00	
TAX	OH	5.5	50.00	50.00	2.75	52.75	
NONTAX	OH-HAM	0	10.00	10.00	0.00	10.00	
TAX	OH-HAM	1	50.00	50.00	0.50	50.50	

Get More Help

Need more assistance with Navision? Get expert help at a reasonable price from the staff at Navision Depot! We are the Navision experts – we've been with Navision from the beginning, and Navision is all we do.

Email to info@navisiondepot.com

or

http://www.navisiondepot.com/navision-consultants.html

With our worldwide network of Navision consultants and developers, we can handle big projects or just answer the occasional question. And since we don't have to support the overhead of a sales force, we are usually much more cost-effective than traditional VARs or Solution Centers.

If this manual, or our other support products, answered your questions, great! If not, please drop us a line, we want to make sure you are 100% satisfied. And if you have any other needs, we'd be delighted to work with you!

Made in the USA
San Bernardino, CA
06 April 2014